UNCOUPLING

The Ugly Truth about Divorce and Finances

UNCOUPLING

The Ugly Truth about Divorce and Finances

A CPA Canada Book

LISA VAN DE GEYN

Cormorant Books

Canadian Heritage / Patrimoine canadien Canada Canada Council for the Arts / Conseil des arts du Canada

 ONTARIO CREATES | ONTARIO CRÉATIF  ONTARIO ARTS COUNCIL / CONSEIL DES ARTS DE L'ONTARIO / an Ontario government agency / un organisme du gouvernement de l'Ontario Ontario

The publisher gratefully acknowledges the support of the Canada Council for the Arts and the
Ontario Arts Council for its publishing program. We acknowledge the financial support of the
Government of Canada through the Canada Book Fund (CBF) for our publishing activities,
and the Government of Ontario through Ontario Creates, an agency of the Ontario Ministry
of Culture, and the Ontario Book Publishing Tax Credit Program.

LIBRARY AND ARCHIVES CANADA CATALOGUING IN PUBLICATION

Title: Uncoupling : the ugly truth about divorce and finances / Lisa van de Geyn.
Names: Van de Geyn, Lisa, author.
Description: "A CPA Canada book."
Identifiers: Canadiana (print) 20220282579 | Canadiana (ebook) 20220282854 |
ISBN 9781770866775 (softcover) | ISBN 9781770866782 (HTML)
Subjects: LCSH: Divorce—Economic aspects—Canada. |
LCSH: Divorced people—Canada—Finance, Personal.
Classification: LCC HG179 .V36 2022 | DDC 332.024086/53—dc23

Cover design: Angel Guerra/Archetype
Interior text design: Tannice Goddard/tannicegdesigns.ca
Printer: Friesens

This book is printed on 100% post-consumer waste recycled paper.

Printed and bound in Canada.

CORMORANT BOOKS INC.
260 SPADINA AVENUE, SUITE 502, TORONTO, ON, M5T 2E4
www.cormorantbooks.com

Contents

The D-Word

DIVORCE IS AN EMOTIONAL ROLLER coaster. We know this; there's no doubt about it. I've witnessed friends, acquaintances, and folks on social media (some whose stories start the chapters that follow — their names and some key details have been changed to protect their identities) go through separation and divorce and they all seem to agree on one thing: how draining the process truly is; how there's so much to understand, prepare, read, gather, act on. That's the impetus for this book. We hope it will serve as a guide to help you embark on this overwhelming journey. Divorce can feel crushing on everything from your emotions to your bank account, but take heart; there are ways in which to get through this time, and we've outlined what you need to know in these six chapters. (Quick note: If you're going through a separation and you're in a common-law relationship, you're also going through an emotional roller coaster. While parts of this book can help you, it's more important that you focus on the laws and regulations in your province or territory that best apply to your specific situation.)

After penning my first book for the Chartered Professional Account-ants of Canada (CPA Canada), *Babies: How to Afford Your Bundle of Joy*, Li Zhang (principal, corporate citizenship) and I were chatting, and she mentioned her interest in doing a book on the ins and outs of divorce. I don't know why the idea appealed to me too, but we started talking about ideas and before I knew it *Uncoupling: The Ugly Truth about Divorce and Finances* was dropped in my hands. This isn't like the book I wrote on the cost of having kids — that was joyous, even if it did remind me how much cash my husband, Peter, and I have spent on our two daughters, Addyson and Peyton. This one was downright nerve-wracking. Who would want to talk about their divorce, and would we be able to pull enough information together to really help someone entering into this distressing stage? Luckily, I found friends, relatives, acquaintances, chartered professional accountants, financial advisers, lawyers, and mediators to be open and honest about their experiences.

In the chapters that follow, you'll find everything from the basics to the nitty-gritty when it comes to separation and divorce, with an emphasis, of course, on finances. As a magazine journalist, I'm no stranger to turning to experts to answer my many (many, many) questions, and the experts I sought are no strangers to talking about all things divorce. They're authorities on everything from specifics about Canada's *Divorce Act* and parenting agreements to the tax implications of divorce and post-divorce to-dos. You'll also hear from one half of various couples who are going through their own separations and divorces. I was empathetic hearing their candid stories — there were plenty of tears, lots of anger, heartache and talk of failure, and unfulfilled dreams. Their stories made me work harder on this book; they made me want to research and offer as much as I could about how to make their financial lives easier while they go through this period of grief.

Here's the thing: not every marriage is a bed of roses. It's not like you fall in love, get engaged, have a beautiful wedding, and immediately start prepping for divorce, but let's be real: not all of us are going to make it when it comes to achieving and maintaining marital bliss. They say fifty percent of marriages ultimately end in saying "I don't." That's a big number.

It wasn't a number Divya was thinking about on the unseasonably warm afternoon in May when she married her tall, dark, handsome Ethan. Overlooking a picturesque lake from her new sister-in-law's yard on the West Coast, Divya and Ethan exchanged their vows while the wind whistled in the trees and their nieces and nephews played tag. (Yes, it was this charming.)

"Before our friends and those special to us here, I Divya, take you, Ethan, as my husband. In friendship and in love, in strength and weakness, in sickness and in health, and for richer or poorer. To share the good times and misfortune, in achievement and failure, to celebrate life with you from this day forward."

It started out smoothly, but it wasn't long before there were more red flags than Divya knew what to do with. Three years and four months later, the words from her vows she remembered most weren't "I do," but "poorer," "misfortune," and "failure." It started as a whirlwind romance, but after the birth of a son the relationship took a turn for the worse. "Our marriage broke down because ultimately, we're not compatible. Our basic values are quite different, and over time, that became crystal clear," thirty-nine-year-old Divya tells me. "My ex said he wanted to be with other people and told me he was unhappy. It wasn't something that could be salvaged."

What happened next isn't the most typical of situations — I don't want to alarm you. A nasty separation ensued — the main issues of contention became parenting time and money. Parenting time ended up being shared equally, which wasn't what Divya necessarily wanted, but it wasn't surprising. Then there was the whole financial aspect. "If I'm being honest, money was always a huge issue for us. He came into the marriage without any and I had significant savings and investments. He liked to shop and spent money like it grew on the maple tree in our front yard. I was a saver — I had been since my first job in high school. We made about the same salary, but he was injured on the job and ended up not working for most of time we were together. Let's just say there was a notable difference in our earnings after that." She's being courteous. There was a serious disparity in their incomes. She was making about $70,000 a year as a registered nurse, while Ethan barely brought in enough to cover his smoking habit. "I think this was a problem for him — he wasn't a consistent provider or even contributor," she says. (It goes without saying that neither Divya nor Ethan read CPA Canada's book *Love and Money: Conversations to Have Before You Get Married* by Wallace M. Howick, FCPA, FCA — it's an important resource that could've helped the two before their relationship got to this toxic point, but I digress. Something else that really would've helped in this intense situation would've been if Divya and Ethan had decided to prepare a marriage contract prior to their nuptials. Again, hindsight is twenty-twenty.) "This was a major issue in our separation and divorce. Both parties are technically supposed to leave the marriage at an 'equal' financial status. This meant I lost all of my savings and money that I brought into the marriage. I had assets — like a car, a house, savings — before I even met him. He didn't contribute to any of those things and wasn't even listed on the mortgage, but after the separation, he was entitled to a significant portion of my financial wealth. It wasn't 'ours' — it was 'mine' before we even moved in together. My father passed away and left me quite a significant amount of money that I used for the down payment on the home I bought that [Ethan] lived in. I lost more than I can say when our marriage ended."

During the nearly four-year-long proceedings, Divya's main concern was her son — she didn't want him to suffer while working out the parenting schedule and other details related to parenting — but she was also burdened with the cost of lawyers. "I tried to avoid using a lawyer and went to a mediator, but Ethan refused to participate in the process, believing the mediator wouldn't be neutral because I'd met her at our consult, which he chose not to show up to. Since then, I've had four lawyers, if you can believe it. I received so much terrible advice. I tried to hire a collaborative lawyer, but Ethan wouldn't get one, so that wasn't an option. Three lawyers either quit or didn't want my case and referred me to others. I had no real understanding of the legal process or what would happen in terms of court proceedings, settlements, etc. There was no collaboration between our lawyers and things dragged on." Once their representation got involved, Divya and Ethan ceased all communication. There were no civil conversations between them, and certainly not about financial issues. "Once a third party is involved in sorting out finances, it basically all goes through a formula, a computer program that calculates everything. Our situation was so bitter and hostile that we didn't discuss anything between us or make any decisions for ourselves. It was all lawyers and formulas, and eventually decided by a judge. And that cost us. In circumstances where you don't get along with your ex, investing in a mediator who can provide help to both parties on an ongoing basis — even for years — is often well worth it. However, both parties have to be willing to come to the table." Divya says she's about $250,000 in debt, paying out both the separation agreement and legal fees. "I'll never be able to financially recover from this."

YES, DIVYA AND ETHAN'S STORY is extreme, but it should serve as required reading for anyone preparing to get hitched. They didn't enter into matrimony believing that a mere forty months after their nuptials they'd be leaving each other. No one does. Still, the fact remains that about forty to fifty percent (or so) of all marriages will end in divorce. Maybe not as bitter a divorce as this couple's, but a divorce, nonetheless.

If you're considering a split in your relationship, you've just found out your spouse wants to call it quits, or you're in the midst of a tough separation, I think the experts and real voices throughout will help. You won't find all the answers to your many questions here (and nothing in this book should be construed as legal advice), but our hope is that you'll at least learn the basics, get some questions answered, and figure out which questions you need to bring to your team of experts. The good news for you is that Divya's and Ethan's messy divorce isn't the norm. There are things you can do and ways to protect yourself against that Hollywood, worst-case-scenario divorce. What's more, we'll help you with your finances along the way, and you'll learn how to better your financial situation post-divorce.

It might feel overwhelming right now, but don't fret. There's plenty of hope for a happy, full, financially stable future.

CHAPTER ONE

My Marriage Is Over

RAJ AND CHRISTINE MET IN university. They were instantly attracted to each other and yes, Raj says "love at first sight" is a fair description of their immediate and intense passion. They were twenty-one and, cliché that it is, they had their whole lives ahead of them, but things moved quickly. They dated for about a year before Raj popped the question. They were married by twenty-three and had their first child, a daughter, at twenty-four. Raj admits those first few years were hard — their decision to get pregnant just months after their wedding meant they weren't like their friends — twenty-somethings who had the freedom to pretty much do whatever their young hearts desired. Raj loved being a father, but it didn't take long before he felt resentful and lost that passion he felt for Christine. He was tired, money was tight, and Christine was often more interested in hanging out with her friends than helping Raj with the kids. By the time he turned thirty — and with three kids at home — Raj says he and Christine were, again, cliché, like two ships passing in the night. They were practically living separate lives under one roof — living apart but together. The financial stress and having three young kids in their twenties really took a toll on their relationship and their whirlwind romance completely fizzled out. They'd never really been friends — they were lovers who "probably rushed into their life together way too quickly," Raj says candidly.

They both knew it was over. Luckily, things were still amicable. Over the course of several heartfelt discussions, they decided their marriage wasn't salvageable — their relationship as husband and wife had fallen apart. There were some hard feelings, of course, but they knew it was time to separate.

It's not easy to admit when your marriage is over. Raj says that even though he knew he wanted a divorce, he worried about their kids — how they'd ever be happy with Mom and Dad living apart. He worried about what he'd say to his colleagues and acquaintances — he had always played the part of the happy husband and father. He worried about money — how would he be able to run a household, let alone pay for childcare, on one salary. Still, he was confident divorce was the right option.

These are all typical worries. Divorce is one of life's most difficult stressors. In fact, on the Holmes-Rahe Stress Inventory, it ranks second to the top stressor — the death of a spouse. It's more stressful than the death of family members, personal illness or injury, losing your job, and even time spent in jail. It's clear that the decision to end a marriage isn't one that's taken lightly, but we know it's one that comes with myriad thoughts, doubts, stresses.

Should You Stay Married or Are You Better Off Divorced?

No one can answer this question for you. It might be worth salvaging and saving, and it might not be. Christine says she had to face the realities of what life would look like divorced and weigh that option against the realities of staying married. For her, the marriage wasn't worth saving.

Since you're the only person who can make this life-altering decision, the experts say there are some questions you should ask yourself. Do you feel like you have nothing left to give to your spouse? Are you out of patience and hope? Do you feel indifference toward your spouse? Has there been a history of abuse, infidelity, or addiction? Does your partner treat you poorly? Is there a total lack of intimacy (affection, emotional intimacy, laughter, and sex)? If you answered "yes" to any of these questions, it might be time to face the music and end your marriage. If you're indifferent or feel detached, it could be a sign that the relationship is over.

If you're seriously contemplating divorce — or you've already made your decision — you're likely going to be feeling nervous, scared, and depressed. These emotions are completely normal. You might want to speak to professionals (think your family doctor, psychologists, and counsellors) about how you're feeling.

Five Things to Do Before You Decide on Divorce

1) Talk to a marriage counsellor or someone who might be able to help you decide whether you want to try to work on any issues with your spouse or separate. If you do this and ultimately decide divorce is your best option, consider divorce counselling, which can help you figure out what went wrong in your marriage and how to pick up the pieces and carry on. There is a lot of shame, fear, guilt, worry, and grief that comes with divorce, and it's something you can receive help with. A trained counsellor or therapist can walk through the process with you and give you an objective point of view — something you'll probably benefit from right now. You can find a professional through your employment benefits, friends, family, or religious leaders.

2) Consult a lawyer with experience in family law in your province or territory. This may not be the person you eventually hire to handle your separation or divorce, but you should start fact-finding as early on as possible so you have an idea of what's coming and what you're up against. There's so much to know about divorce and no matter where you live across Canada, there are complex laws that can be confusing when you're already dealing with a ton of stress. It's best to find out about your options early on, so you have time to consider what road you'll take and possible outcomes. This part is as easy as googling "lawyer in [your city]." Start there.

3) Ask the lawyer about leaving the home you share with your spouse, if that's something that's been on your mind. Don't just leave without seeking advice, especially if there are children involved. There can be consequences to leaving your home in non-violent circumstances and it could create further financial burden through the divorce. That said, if your spouse is violent and abusive, your primary responsibility is to protect yourself and your kids. Depending on where you live, there are various organizations that provide relief for people escaping abusive relationships and, once you feel safe, they may be able to put you in touch with lawyers or other professionals to assist you.

4) Start protecting yourself financially. If divorce is imminent, open your own bank account, apply for your own credit card and check your credit rating. You should consider seeking legal advice, however, if you plan to make a significant change to the financial status quo prior to resolving any financial issues. Consistently checking your credit rating is a good habit to have. These are elements you should have regardless of a divorce as they are critical for financial independence.

5) Start getting your financial affairs in order. The more you prepare, the easier and more efficient it will be to resolve any financial issues, which may save you money later. Know what your financial position will be and gather all the paperwork listing your own assets and debts, including your tax documents. In general, both parties are required to provide full financial disclosure of any assets held in their name and in joint names.

Coping With Separation and Divorce

- Validate your feelings. You'll have a host of different feelings — we're talking anything from anxiety and grief to shame and depression. Understand that this is completely normal. It's okay to feel sad, angry, confused, and tired. And it's okay for these feelings to be super intense. The good news is that with some help, a supportive circle, and doing some research, these feelings won't be quite as intense over time.

- Be kind to yourself. Give yourself a break — divorce is a big deal. It's perfectly understandable to find it difficult to function at your normal level. This is a setback and it's one that will take time, effort, and energy to heal from.
- Create a strong support circle. Yes, we're talking about everyone from your parents and siblings to friends and close colleagues. It takes a village. Not only should you share your feelings with your close circle, you should also consider speaking to a therapist or psychologist to help you come to terms with this tough period in your life. Don't isolate — it's much healthier to talk it out and get support.
- If you have children, check in with them. Make sure they are provided with coping tools and mechanisms to help them adjust to a new reality. If you think your children need additional support from professionals and you've already separated, you should try to agree with your ex about an appropriate program before enrolling the children.

Preparing Your Finances as You Plan for Separation

Most couples enter marriage assuming their marriages will last "until death do us part," and don't usually plan on separating from their partner, and therefore don't plan on going from a dual-income to a single-income household. In most dual-income households, the budget is prepared assuming both partners will share the costs of operating a home. If you are planning on separating from your spouse, you will no longer be able to rely on his or her income, and chances are this will result in your income not being enough to cover all your current household expenses. More often than not, this will lead to major cash-flow problems after separation.

Of course, the ideal is to live within your means after you separate, which means spending less than you earn. The best time to start thinking about these issues is before you start the process of separating and divorcing.

Understanding Your Spending Habits

Given that you'll no longer have your spouse's income to depend on, you'll need to track your expenses to better understand how you're spending money so you can find out how to reduce your costs once you become separated. There are many free options offered by the big Canadian banks that help you automatically track your income and expenses, such as:

BMO
- A free service offered to BMO (Bank of Montreal) everyday banking and MasterCard customers that tracks your spending and allows you to set up budgets, etc.
- www.bmo.com/moneylogic

TD
- TD MySpend categorizes and monitors your spending, providing a daily update of the day's transactions. It also provides insights into your spending to give you a picture of how you're spending as compared to the past.

Overall, one of the most important steps you can take when planning your finances for a separation is to start developing the habit of budgeting and tracking your spending. This is a crucial step; if you neglect it, your spending can quickly get out of control, forcing you into a tough financial situation. Budgeting and planning are key at this point in your life.

Analyze Your Cash Flow

Don't worry — this sounds much more daunting than it is. After you figure out how you're spending your money, you can use the following guide to analyze and plan your cash flow in advance of separating.

Over the next twelve months, write down:

- Basic expenses: These are "needs" (as opposed to "wants"). They include your mortgage or rent, utilities, insurance payments, debt repayment (including line of credit payments), RRSP contributions, medical or dental care, property taxes, transportation costs, groceries, and clothing.

- Other expenses: These are your "wants," and they include the "nice-to-have" clothing, meals out, manicures and pedicures, sports tickets, having coffee out, entertainment, gifts, vacations, etc. Once you separate, you might also want to put money aside to join social groups. There are lots of support and social groups recently separated individuals can join; some are free, but many require a fee to join and participate.

- Using a template from the internet, financial institution, or creating your own budget sheet (like the one highlighted at the end of this section) will help give you an idea of what you can trim from your spending. Want to save some money before you separate? Start practicing picking up a coffee twice a week rather than every day, or cancel some of those online subscriptions that you never use.

- Chances are you won't be able to cut all the expenses you'll need to before you separate, but you can work on trimming your costs and start to plan how to cut those larger expenses.

- Next, do some planning and calculate how much you'll get from your different sources of income, employment, and income from businesses you own. Once you separate, chances are you will lose the income of your partner and will want to think of ways to supplement some of that lost income, such as through a side hustle. I'd caution against including any amount you expect to receive in the form of child support and/or spousal support at this stage since no separation agreement has been finalized and signed.

- After comparing your expected household income to your expenses, you're likely to find you'll need to make adjustments to your spending habits, so it makes sense to start cutting some expenses and test driving your new budget as much as possible in order to practice living on a reduced income to see how you manage.

- Finally, the big elephant in the room will be your housing situation and expenses after you separate, especially because housing costs are the largest expense for most households. Will you be able to afford your current home on a reduced income? Will you need to think about renting a portion of your home to generate some additional income? Is that even a possibility? Are you comfortable renting out your home? At this stage you won't need to make a final decision on this question, particularly since a separation agreement isn't signed, but these are all things you'll want to think about.

Budget Template

To access and complete your own budget worksheet, please see the worksheet included below or visit www.cpacanada.ca/finlitresources, under money management worksheets, to download your own worksheet. Alternatively, you can also create an online budget worksheet by visiting the Ontario Securities Commission website: www.getsmarter aboutmoney.ca/calculators/cash-flow-calculator.

Monthly Income	
Salary after taxes (take-home pay, self-employment/business income)	$
Other income (e.g., investment income)	$
Total Income	$

Monthly Expenses — Fixed	
Housing costs (e.g., mortgage, rent, condo/maintenance fees, property taxes, etc.)	$
Utilities — heat, hydro, water	$
Services — phone, cable/satellite, internet, security system	$
Insurance — auto, home, life, disability	$

Monthly Expenses — Fixed cont'd	
Child care	$
Existing loans and credit cards (minimum monthly payments)	$
Other fixed expenses (e.g., child support, alimony, etc.)	$
Total Expenses — Fixed	$

Monthly Expenses — Variable	
Groceries	$
Household maintenance (e.g., renovations, landscaping and gardening, housecleaning, snow removal, lawn care, etc.)	$
Transportation (e.g., car lease, gas, transit, car service and repairs, parking fees, licence and registration, etc.)	$
Uninsured health services (e.g., prescriptions, dental care, eye care, counselling, any other health services not covered under a plan)	$
Education (e.g., tuition, books, exam fees, etc.)	$
Long-term savings (e.g., monthly pension plan and registered savings plans like RRSPs, TFSAs, and RESPs)	$
Other variable expenses	$
Total Expenses — Variable	$

Monthly Expenses — Discretionary	
Personal (e.g., clothing, shoes, gifts, salon, gym membership, etc.)	$
Daily living (e.g., pet expenses, dry cleaning, etc.)	$
Entertainment (e.g., dining out, movies, music, theatre/concerts, etc.)	$
Donations	$
Vacation	$
Other discretionary expenses	$
Total Expenses — Discretionary	$

Monthly Cash Flow	
Total Income	$
Total Expenses (Fixed, Variable, and Discretionary)	$
Net Cash Flow (Total Income — Total Expenses)	$

Seek Out Financial Advice

As you start to plan out your financial life after you separate, it's wise to seek advice from a qualified finance professional to figure out the best options available to you based on your own facts and circumstances.

I've Made Up My Mind. I Want a Divorce. Now What?

You've made the decision. What happens after you decide your marriage is over? Russell Alexander is the founder and senior partner of Russell Alexander Collaborative Family Lawyers. The firm has seven offices across Ontario, with their base of operations in Lindsay. Since 1998, Alexander has helped people deal with pretty much every divorce scenario. He says his clients call him "wanting to know that they're going to be okay — they want to know they'll enjoy the same lifestyle they did during the marriage. They want to know they'll have a home and continue to have a good relationship with their children, and they want to know what's fair, but they don't know because they don't know the law." He says it's typical for someone who is contemplating divorce to speak to their family doctor, religious leader, counsellor, friends, and family about their decision. From there, it's best to be referred to a lawyer whom they know or who has worked with family, a friend, or colleague before. "You typically make an appointment to meet to tell the lawyer your story. Lots of lawyers are active listeners, though some are more structured and want to do an analysis right away," he explains. The most important part of this meeting, says Alexander, is explaining your goals and interests. For most families, children will be at the top of their list. "Then the lawyer will give you an explanation of the process. How you go through the process from start to finish. There are lots of ways to do this. The most common way in Canada is for the lawyer to reach out to the other spouse and tell him or her to get a lawyer, then the two lawyers can work out a resolution, which inevitably turns into the separation agreement." It's not atypical for the lawyers to work on this together, or for both spouses to be involved, though in the instance of domestic violence or abuse, it may not be appropriate to have everyone in the same room.

Jessica Chapman is a lawyer in Dartmouth, Nova Scotia. She says there are some things clients can have ready when they make that first call, including a list of their assets and debts in their name, as well as assets and debts held jointly and those of the other party, if they have access to it. "It's also helpful to know what their income is, because in family-law matters, whether you're the payer or the recipient, your income becomes relevant. Not knowing this can cause more work for the lawyer," she says. "The other thing I would suggest before you meet with a lawyer is to really put some thought into what you want. It may be that you don't know, and that's okay, but if someone says, 'We've just separated and this is what's happening,' and I ask, 'What is it that you want out of this? What are your priorities? What parenting arrangement do you think is best for your kids?' If the answer is 'I don't know' to any of those questions, it makes it very difficult for me to create a strategy on their file. I say this is the ideal because people start this process at different times in their grieving process. I've met with clients who are planning to leave their spouse and who are very early on in processing all of this, and I've had clients retain me who have been separated for fifteen years and this is just a formality and they've never signed anything and want it done now. So, when I say 'ideally,' those people who have very recently separated, lawyers can't expect them to have the wherewithal to be the most prepared they can possibly be because it is, for a lot of people, one of the most difficult life circumstances they've found themselves in. A lot of people are just looking for general information so they can figure out what it is they do want. You won't find a lot of family lawyers who will require all of this because it's a lot to ask, depending on circumstances."

A typical question is "How long will this separation take?" Chapman says this always depends on the parties. "There is a great variety in terms of how long your separation could take to be finalized and it's usually based on the reasonableness of the parties and how much the parties are on the same page with what their expectations are," she says, adding she often tells clients that family law is about lawyers helping with what is otherwise a very personal matter. "So, in your best-case scenario, you have two reasonable people who are both at stages at the end of their relationship where they're able to sit down at the kitchen table and figure out what works for the family. The best-case scenario is I have a client who calls me and says, 'We talked it out and this is what we're thinking. What do you think and what does the law say about this? Am I giving up on anything too big? If not, can you just draft this up and we'll sign it.' Best-case is everyone is reasonable and on the same page and wants to be fair.

"There are a lot of emotions though. People are going through a massive identity shift. What they thought their future looked like has changed and the rest of their life looks much different now. In addition to grieving the relationship, they're also dealing with grieving what they thought the future would be like for them. Worst-case scenario is they end up being my client for five-plus years because they can't agree on anything, and we have to go through the court process and a full-blown trial."

Alexander and Chapman both encourage their clients to resolve issues outside of the court system. "Your lawyer will know fairly quickly whether or not it can be settled outside of court. If one spouse makes crazy demands or ignores letters from the other lawyer, it would be necessary to take them to court to get a judge to make an order," Alexander says.

Chapman adds that while more files are collaborative, going to court is still common. "There are people who aren't going to be on the same page and court intervention is simply necessary. I have seen the toll going to court takes on people, so I almost always advise settling, even if it means you might not get as much as you would've gotten in court before a judge. It's not just the tens of thousands of dollars you pay a law firm to prepare and attend a trial, it's the sleepless nights and preparing to be cross-examined on the stand and under oath by a lawyer — it's all of the stress of having your dirty laundry aired. In some cases, you also still have to be prepared to deal with the other party in a co-parenting capacity for what could be many years. Kids can sense that conflict and that conflict reaches an all-time high when you're going the court route for a hearing. Court intervention depends on the file but personally, as all lawyers should in family law, I very much encourage settlement when appropriate," she says.

Let's say I want a divorce. In an ideal world, I'd find a lawyer recommended to me by friends or family. I'd call them, explain my situation and my thinking, and they would describe next steps. The lawyer would reach out to my spouse's lawyer, who would respond and, together, they'd schedule a date to go through our case. "We'll decide whether we'll work with mediation, arbitration, go the collaborative family law route, or ask a judge to make an order. We go the judge route if, say, your spouse refuses to pay child or spousal support, refuses to divide their pension, if they have a drug or alcohol addiction and are unable to parent responsibly, if they aren't prepared to disclose their financial assets, or if we're trying to preserve their assets so they don't run away to Las Vegas with a new partner," says Alexander.

Pre-divorce Financial/Document Check

Now's the time to get yourself organized. This is a tough, emotional time, but you'll do yourself a favour if you spend some time gathering the documents you need to proceed with separation and divorce.

Legal documents
- Driver's licence/passport/citizenship documents
- Personal information, including: both spouses' full legal name; date of birth; Social Insurance Number; date of separation/projected date; length of cohabitation/marriage; current living arrangements; occupations; name and address of employers; most recent annual income tax return and Notice of Assessment
- Children's birth certificates

- Marriage certificate (this should be the original); if the original is misplaced a replica can usually be ordered from the municipality in which you were married
- Marriage contract (sometimes this is referred to as a prenuptial agreement) (if applicable)

Financial documents
- Photocopy or scan all necessary paperwork, such as those listed below:
  - Investment and insurance statements for both spouses (this includes all Registered Retirement Savings Plans, Registered Education Savings Plans, Tax-Free Savings Accounts, and non-registered investment accounts)
  - Tax returns and Notices of Assessment (NOA) for both spouses for the last three years (you can download your NOA from your CRA account if you have activated My Account)
  - If you're self-employed, ensure you have necessary documents pertaining to the business (there may be additional disclosure requirements for people who are self-employed. You should consult with a lawyer to ensure you are meeting your disclosure obligations)
  - Current and end-of-year pay stubs for both spouses
  - Beneficiaries for Registered Retirement Savings Plans, pensions, Tax-Free Savings Accounts and Registered Education Savings Plans
  - Canada Pension Plan statements (and any other national pension statements, if applicable)
  - Pension statements
  - Group benefit books from your employer(s)
  - For those who have already claimed pension: documents regarding the options you chose at retirement and annual statement
  - Property valuations or tax notices for real estate each spouse owns individually or jointly
  - Digital assets, such as cryptocurrencies, credit card rewards, digital wallets

Debts, banking and spending
- Photocopy or scan statements for all debts, such as:
  - Mortgage, credit cards, car loans, lines of credit, education debt, etc.; find the name of the financial institution, balance owing, interest rate and amortization, monthly payment amount
  - Debts you've co-signed for or guaranteed for family, friend, or company (if applicable)
  - Recent banking statements
  - Joint debt: find out what controls, if any, are in place so that debt doesn't mount without your consent
  - Credit card statements: if you don't have a separate bank account or credit card, consider opening one
  - Spending on children (document what you spend on children's expenses, including extra-curricular activities, clothes, lessons, dental, medical, etc.)

Personal assets
- If you have art, antiques, jewellery or other high-value collections, get appraisals or insured value for each
- Ownership papers for cars and any other vehicles

Insurance including life, disability, long-term care, and critical illness
- Collect copies of all policies and gather costs and beneficiaries on each
- Search bank statements for payments of premiums — could be monthly, or more likely annually
- Ask lawyer how and when beneficiaries can be updated

Medical insurance
- If covered under spouse's plan, consider other options of coverage available to you, including via your employer or buying your own coverage
- Ensure all health claims have been submitted and claimed

Corporations/businesses
- If either spouse owns a business, get appropriate partnership agreements, incorporation and registration documents
- Provide the last three years of tax returns or relevant tax schedules for the business
- Are there business debts that have been co-signed or guaranteed by either spouse?
- Are there assets owned by the business (such as cars or real estate)?
- Provide the last three years of financial statements
- Often a spouse will need to have a business valuation performed on their business, depending on the type of business

Housing
- If you're moving, start researching the cost of renting or owning. Don't commit to anything until you speak to your accountant or another financial adviser

Special circumstances
- Speak to your lawyer and financial adviser if you:
  - care for physically disabled people
  - care for dependent parents
  - have children with learning or other disabilities
  - have children from another relationship (or if your spouse does)
  - received an inheritance during the marriage

Budget work
- What is your current budget?
- What do your post-divorce cash flow needs look like? What are your sources of income? What expenses do you have?
- Talk to a licenced financial professional about your budget and how to get financial assistance if needed

Parenting Considerations

You should consider what you are hoping for in terms of parenting arrangements so that when you sit down with your ex-spouse (or lawyer) to work out details, you have an idea of your goals. There are a lot of different details to consider. As you do so, remember that this can be a difficult and emotional process and you may consider consulting your family doctor or a counsellor, as well as your accountant and/or financial advisers to make sure you are getting the best possible advice.

Parenting Schedules and Living Arrangements

- Housing arrangements — will you both stay in the same house, move between homes, or is there another arrangement that works best for your family? Take geography into consideration — parents may want to remain close in proximity so there's less travel time to see children, kids can remain in their school district and near their friends, etc.
- How will parenting time be shared? Be sure you've discussed special days, such as birthdays, holidays, weddings, and vacation time with your ex-spouse to decrease the chances of arguments in the future.
- Consider how you'll manage changes to the parenting time schedule. (For example, what will happen if there are illnesses, lateness, and unforeseen events.) How much notice will be required and will there be make-up time with the parent?
- How will childcare and babysitting arrangements work?
- Will the children's belongings be moved between homes or will they have separate sets of clothes and personal items, for example, at each parent's home?
- How will you deal with children's social time with friends and social events? Who will take kids to birthday parties, for example?

Decision-making responsibility generally includes major decisions in a child's life, like healthcare, education, and religion. In general, responsibility for these broad areas is shared, but depending on a child's and family's needs, parents may agree to split responsibility in various ways.

Healthcare

- Who will be the main decision-maker when it comes to medical and dental care, or will this be shared? If shared, how will decisions be made if parents don't agree?
- Who will be responsible for medical and dental checkups?
- Who will care for children when they're ill?
- Will kids be covered under both parents' medical insurance?
- If required, who will make arrangements for supplies, medication, or equipment needed?

Education and Significant Extracurriculars

- How will decisions be made about educational needs, change in school, tutoring, etc.?
- Who will attend school trips, parent-teacher conferences, school events?
- Who will be the main parent contact on file at school?
- Will consent be needed before one parent enrolls kids in extracurricular activities? Who will pay for equipment? If one parent insists on putting a child into ice hockey, will the ex-spouse have to fund a portion of the costs?
- Who can attend extracurricular activities? Can a parent attend extracurricular activities on the other parent's time to watch?

Religion and Culture

- How will the kids be brought up?
- What religion and culture will the kids be brought up in?
- What religious and cultural activities, and types of education will be permitted?
- Will the kids learn another language?

Travel

- What kind of notice and consent is necessary prior to travelling to any location with children within Canada?
- What will be the procedure for obtaining notarized consent to travel out of country? (The Canadian government strongly

recommends Canadian children — anyone under the age of eighteen or nineteen, depending on your province — travel with a consent letter if they're travelling abroad alone, with one parent or guardian, with friends or relatives, or with a group. The letter serves as a clear sign that the child has permission to travel abroad from parents or guardians who are *not* accompanying them on their trip. You can get templates for travel letters at www.travel.gc.ca/travelling/children/consent-letter.)

- Who will be the custodian of the kids' passports? Who will store the passports?

Parent Communication
- What type of information will be communicated?
- How will you communicate — email, text, phone, parenting communication app?
- How will emergency communications be handled?

Problem-Solving
- How will disputes be rectified and resolved? Via mediation? Counsellor? Lawyer?

Other Parenting Issues
- Discipline
- Internet-use and use of electronic devices and phones (including social media presence). How will you determine who pays for the device and phone plan?
- Diet and nutrition
- Gifts
- Family pets
- What will happen when parents have new partners?

Divorce: The Basics

What is divorce? Divorce is the legal process married couples must go through to end their marriage. Only married couples can get a divorce and only a court can grant one. When the divorce is finalized, a divorce certificate proves you're no longer married. (Separation is different — there's no formal process to file for separation and no legal status for separation. In the case of separation, you basically separate and your date of separation — which isn't always agreed upon — serves as the valuation date.)

How do I get a divorce in Canada? You need to submit an application to a court in the province or territory where you or your spouse lives — it is the provincial or territorial government's responsibility for making rules about divorce in their jurisdiction. So, application forms and procedures vary from one province or territory to the next. Visit these sites in your province or territory for specific details:

Alberta: www.alberta.ca/family-law-assistance.aspx
British Columbia: www2.gov.bc.ca/gov/content/life-events/divorce/ family-justice
Manitoba: www.gov.mb.ca/justice/crown/family/law/
New Brunswick: www.familylawnb.ca/
Newfoundland & Labrador: www.court.nl.ca/supreme/family-division/ info-common-legal-issues/divorce-and-separation/

Nova Scotia: www.nsfamilylaw.ca/
Northwest Territories: www.justice.gov.nt.ca/en/browse/children-and-families/
Nunavut: www.gov.nu.ca/programs/justice
Ontario: www.attorneygeneral.jus.gov.on.ca/english/family/
Prince Edward Island: www.princeedwardisland.ca/en/topic/family-law
Quebec: www.justice.gouv.qc.ca/en/couples-and-families/
Saskatchewan: www.saskatchewan.ca/residents/births-deaths-marriages-and-divorces/separation-or-divorce

Yukon: yukon.ca/en/legal-and-social-supports/family-law

Do I need a reason to get a divorce? Yes, you need to show that your marriage has broken down in one of three ways:

- you and your spouse have separated and lived apart for at least a year (this is known as a no-fault divorce; more on this later);
- your spouse has been mentally or physically cruel to you, making it intolerable to live together; or
- your spouse has committed adultery (these are known as for-fault divorces).

How long do I have to wait before applying? It depends on what you're claiming. You can apply at any time if your marriage has broken down because of mental and/or physical cruelty, or because of adultery. If the reason is because you've separated, you need to show you have been living apart for one year before your divorce can be granted. The caveat here is that even if you live apart for a year, a divorce is not granted until all matters (these are financial and parenting issues, if applicable) within the filing are addressed and agreed upon.

Your Legal Rights and Obligations (Example from Ontario's Ministry of the Attorney General) — Make Sure to Consult Your Own Provincial/Territorial Laws

1) Staying in the family home. Married people both have an equal right to stay in the home regardless of how title is held, unless a judge decides that one of you must leave. You cannot decide to sublet, rent, sell, or mortgage it without the other's permission (even if the home is in your name). If you both want to stay in the family home and you can't agree on who should stay, you can use lawyers, a mediator, or an arbitrator to decide. (More on the family or matrimonial home in Chapter 3.)

2) Caring for the kids. Both parents should be responsible for their children's upbringing. Period. However, in the world of divorce, this is only true if there is shared decision-making. You are still responsible to provide your kids with a safe and loving place to live, food, and clothing. Your children should be kept safe. If you and your spouse are amicable, you can write a parenting plan together — this includes when each parent will spend time with the kids and who makes major decisions when it comes to their

wellbeing. This can be part of your separation agreement. If you can't agree on a parenting schedule, or on who will make decisions about the children, a judge can decide in court. (Judges might ask for professionals such as social workers, psychologists, or psychiatrists to provide assessments.) The children's best interest is the only consideration for a judge when making a decision about parenting. However, a history of violence or abuse in the relationship or house should be brought to the judge's attention as that is one factor, among others, that will help a judge determine what is in a child's best interests. It is important to recognize that there is a difference between parenting time (the time-sharing arrangement between parents) and decision-making responsibility (who makes the major decisions affecting a child). Regardless of how the parenting time is shared, if there is joint decision-making, both parents have the right to contribute to major decisions about their children's health, education, religion, and other important matters.

3) Financially supporting your children. Again, both parents are responsible for this — responsibility is shared when families are living together and it continues to be shared when parents separate. Depending on the income levels and the amount of parenting time that each parent has, one parent may have to pay child support to assist in equalizing the children's standard of living between the homes. The amount of child support paid in a province such as Ontario is set out in the Child Support Guidelines; please check your appropriate provincial/territorial resources (link available in the glossary/resources section). However, in exceptional circumstances the court can order an amount that's higher or lower than the guidelines. More on support in Chapter 5.

4) Financially supporting your spouse. There's usually one person at an economic disadvantage during a relationship. (For example, one person usually spends more time looking after the children and might not have the ability to earn a lot of money in the workforce.) The law sees spousal relationships as economic partnerships, and when the partnership breaks down, the person who earns more money may have to support the other. To figure out whether spousal

support is necessary, a judge first determines whether one spouse was at an economic disadvantage because of the marriage. The judge then looks at the relative incomes of the parties to determine the amount of support. The duration of spousal support must also be determined. The goal of the law is for the person seeking support to become self-sufficient as quickly as possible. The general rule of thumb is people who have been together for a short time only get support for the short term. If one person in the relationship has spent years out of the workforce or years working lower-paying jobs, their former partner might have to pay longer-term support. There are various criteria taken into consideration when determining the appropriate amount and duration of spousal support including things like the age and health of the couple, number of years married, available employment opportunities, the contribution made to family care during the relationship, the family's standard of living pre-separation, and the time it will take to become self-sufficient. More on spousal support in Chapter 5.

5) Dividing your property. The law says a marriage is an equal partnership, and when it's over, the property acquired during the marriage must be divided. The general rule is the value of any property you acquired during your marriage that you still have when you separate must be divided equally, fifty-fifty. It is important to note that it is the *value* of the property that is being shared and that, absent an agreement to the contrary, you are not generally required to transfer title or physically transfer property to your ex-spouse. Property you brought into your marriage is yours to keep, but any increase in the value of this property during your marriage must be shared. You'll learn about the exceptions to this rule in Chapter 3. The family home is an exception to the general rules, too. You'll also learn about that in Chapter 3.

Steps to Take for Divorce

Step 1: Make the decision to separate from your spouse. Determining that you're ready to separate is a big decision that starts the process. At the outset, you'll be wondering what this will look like logistically and financially — where are you going to live and how will you support yourself (and any children) on one income. It's best to figure out your living and financial situations as early as you can so you can focus on the remaining factors of the separation or divorce. If you have children, you'll also be thinking about parenting arrangements. If your goal is to share parenting time equally with your spouse, it will be to your benefit to work with your ex or soon-to-be ex-spouse to find ways to share the day-to-day parenting responsibilities to minimize the disruption to the children's lives once the divorce is final.

Step 2: Get a divorce application. You'll find each province and territory has their own forms, so you'll need to file accordingly based on where you live. You can obtain the forms from a lawyer, court office, or bookstore.

Step 3: What are your grounds for filing for divorce? Is it for-fault or no-fault? Fault divorces are filed under the grounds of cruelty or adultery. You must be able to provide evidence of either. No-fault divorces require a one-year separation period.

No-fault divorces: You don't have to be separated for a year to apply for a divorce, but the divorce won't be granted until the one-year period has lapsed. This doesn't mean you need to be physically separated — that is, live in separate houses — from your spouse. It does mean you have to be living separate lives for a year. If you're living in the same home (for the kids or financial reasons), you'll have to show the court that even though you live together, you aren't living as a couple. Most experts say you should get legal assistance if you find yourself in this situation as it can be difficult to prove you're maintaining separate lives.

If you end up getting back together and then want to separate, you don't necessarily have to start the one-year separation period again — but if you were together for more than ninety days, you'll have to restart. The purpose of this is to give couples a chance to work on repairing their relationship without delaying a divorce if it doesn't work out.

The no-fault divorce is generally the least complicated and least expensive way to get a divorce in Canada.

For-fault divorces: This type of divorce means that one spouse is attempting to show that the other spouse is fully at fault for the dissolution of the marriage. Courts do need proof to substantiate the claim, and you generally need legal representation or assistance to go this route. These divorces are expensive, they take longer than uncontested divorces, and they're not easy — this is a difficult road to go down and it might take more than a year to be processed.

Step 4: Figure out whether your divorce is uncontested or contested.

Uncontested divorces: Each spouse agrees to the reasons behind the divorce. This requires one application.

Contested divorces: Spouses disagree on the reasons behind the divorce. This requires each spouse filing a separate application.

Step 5: If you have children, you must include an overview of the arrangements you have made for your children, including parenting and support.

Step 6: You must file your application at a courthouse or via your lawyer. Depending on your province or territory, there are fees to apply and formalities that must be followed. A lawyer can assist you with this.

Step 7: You'll receive clearance from the Canadian Divorce Registry. When divorce papers are served to your spouse, they have thirty days to respond to the application.

Step 8: If your spouse doesn't respond in thirty days, you can continue the divorce process by submitting your Affidavit for Divorce, Divorce Order, and Clerk's Certificate to the court. If your spouse does respond, you have to wait for the court to grant your divorce. A Divorce Order is issued when a judge is satisfied with the information you've submitted.

Step 9: You'll get your Certificate of Divorce about thirty-one days after the Divorce Order is granted by the court. Now you're legally divorced in Canada.

Common Questions:

Q: **What happens if we try to reconcile and live together again?**

A: If you've applied for divorce based on a one-year separation, you have up to ninety days if you're trying to reconcile. If it doesn't work out, you can continue your action for a divorce as if you had never spent this ninety-day period as a couple.

Q: **What if we have kids?**

A: Your best bet is to agree on child support and parenting arrangements. You can ask the court to make orders on these issues as part of your divorce proceedings. A court can only grant your divorce if it's satisfied that reasonable arrangements have been made for any children.

Q: **Can I get a divorce if my ex and I haven't decided on certain issues such as our parenting schedule?**

A: Yes, you can start an application for divorce or, if one has already been started, you can bring a motion to ask for a divorce order. Be aware that the court might not grant you the divorce before other issues are decided. For example, if you have kids, a court won't grant you a divorce until you've shown you've made an arrangements for any children.

Q: **I've lived with my partner for years, but we're not married. Do we need a formal divorce?**

A: No, only married people need a divorce. That said, people who have lived together may have other issues that need to be decided, including decision-making, parenting time, support, and division of jointly owned property. Speak to a lawyer about your rights if you're in a common-law relationship that is ending.

Q: **What if I can't afford a lawyer?**

A: Your province or territory will likely have family justice services, such as mediation, to help you and your spouse work out some or all issues before court. You might also qualify for legal aid, depending on your province and income. Engaging a lawyer does not necessarily need to be an all or nothing affair. Depending on where you live, many lawyers offer unbundled legal services, meaning that they can assist you with discrete tasks rather than managing your case from start to finish.

Q: **Can I represent myself in court?**

A: Technically yes, but the short answer is you shouldn't take this route. Family law is hard, and not only will you need to understand the laws that apply to your situation, you'll also need to be well-versed in court procedures in your province or territory. You should consult a lawyer before deciding. Your province or territory might have a lawyer referral service that can refer you to a family law lawyer who might offer a brief consultation for free or at a reduced rate.

Q: **When does a divorce take effect?**

A: Divorce generally takes effect thirty-one days after the judge grants it. You can request a divorce certificate confirming the divorce and the date it took effect. If you are basing your divorce on the grounds of adultery or cruelty and the court is satisfied that the grounds exist, then your divorce could be granted immediately. To get a copy of the certificate, you need to contact the court that processed the divorce.

Q: **What factors will a court take into account when considering what is in the child's best interest for the allocation of parenting time?**

A: There is no one-size-fits-all approach to family situations — family dynamics are diverse. However, the Divorce Act gives effect to what is sometimes referred to as the "maximum contact principle" which states that when "allocating parent time, the court shall give effect to the principle that a child should have as much time with each spouse as is consistent with the best interests of the child." In determining the best interests of the child, the court shall consider all factors related to the circumstances of the child, including:

    a) the child's needs, given the child's age and stage of development, such as the child's need for stability;

b) the nature and strength of the child's relationship with each spouse, each of the child's siblings and grandparents and any other person who plays an important role in the child's life;

c) each spouse's willingness to support the development and maintenance of the child's relationship with the other spouse;

d) the history of care of the child;

e) the child's views and preferences, giving due weight to the child's age and maturity, unless they cannot be ascertained;

f) the child's cultural, linguistic, religious and spiritual upbringing and heritage, including Indigenous upbringing and heritage;

g) any plans for the child's care;

h) the ability and willingness of each person in respect of whom the order would apply to care for and meet the needs of the child;

i) the ability and willingness of each person in respect of whom the order would apply to communicate and cooperate, in particular with one another, on matters affecting the child;

j) any family violence and its impact on, among other things,

    i) the ability and willingness of any person who engaged in the family violence to care for and meet the needs of the child, and

    ii) the appropriateness of making an order that would require persons in respect of whom the order would apply to cooperate on issues affecting the child;

k) any civil or criminal proceeding, order, condition, or measure that is relevant to the safety, security and well-being of the child.

Q: Can other family members be granted access to children?

A: As part of the need for the "best interest of the child," the Act allows non-parents (grandparents and other close family members) to apply for the right to spend a certain amount of time with the children. If granted, a legally binding "contact order" is entered with the court.

Q: What is a separation agreement?

A: Also known as a divorce agreement, this is a legal contract between spouses with regards to all issues — including financial and parenting agreements — going forward. (This isn't the document that ends your marriage. Depending on where you live, you'll have to apply for a divorce decree to officially call it quits.) You need a separation agreement to ensure support and to protect your assets and interests. In fact, this is often called the most important legal document you'll sign because it will define the terms between you and your former spouse.

You'll want to make a separation agreement because:
- it's a legal contract that records the terms of your agreement;
- it can be enforced by the court;
- it's cheaper than going to court;
- it can help avoid any confusion (and believe us, there's often lots of confusion) over what to do about certain family-law issues after you separate.

Separation agreements include:
- full financial disclosure
- a settlement of parenting arrangements
- child support obligations and guidelines
- spousal support obligations
- valuation of pensions, including government pensions, such as Canadian Pension Plan (CPP) benefits
- division of assets and debts
- tax obligations
- separation of the matrimonial home
- a future dispute resolution clause
- any independent legal advice

The agreement must follow certain rules to make it enforceable under the law; it's made to give the court power to order you and your ex-partner to do exactly what the agreement says in the event that one of you stops following it. For example, when it comes to dividing property, you and your former partner must tell each other about all of your finances (this is called financial disclosure). If you don't, you're in breach of the law and your separation agreement.

It's in your best interest to have your separation agreement drafted by your lawyer.

Here are some of the types of information you may need for your separation agreement:

- Full legal name of you and your spouse
- Your date of separation
- Issues regarding children, including who they'll live with, parenting arrangements, who has access, how much child support will be paid, how family vacations will be covered, etc.
- Issues regarding spousal support, including whether it will be paid, how much, for how long, etc.
- Property division, including a list dividing which items each of you are to receive and when. If you own a home, you'll need to include information about whether it will be sold, who's responsible for it until it's sold, who lives in it until it's sold, and how the sale proceeds will be divided
- Debts, including who's responsible for which debts and how debts incurred after separation (but before divorce) will be handled
- Registered Retirement Savings Plans, Registered Education Savings Plans and government and private pensions, including whether you'll split these plans or pensions

Q: What is financial disclosure?

A: This is the exchange of information about your finances. It is done by completing a financial disclosure form on which you list your assets and liabilities at various points in time, usually on the date of marriage, the date of separation, and at present. This is where you lay it all out when it comes to disclosing your assets, which include things like pensions, investments, insurance benefits, real estate, and savings — it means a lot of digging for credit reports, property deeds, bank statements, and other key financial forms. You'll also have to declare your debts the day you were married, the day you separated, and at present time.

Full financial disclosures will need to be made before a settlement can be negotiated because all parties need to know where their finances stand in an open, transparent manner. This is the way in which you'll be making financial decisions moving forward. That's why these documents must be accurate — you cannot provide estimations during this process. This is why it is important to be an active participant in your finances on a daily basis to have a clear understanding of what the assets are and also where the assets and documentation are located. If you think your spouse may hide assets or make it difficult for you to obtain this information, it would be important for you to get this paperwork in order before you start divorce proceedings.

The kinds of documents you'll need to prepare are:
- Account statements and bank balances
- Property values
- Mortgage statements
- Loan and debt statements
- GICs and RRSP verifications
- TFSAs and other investment accounts you hold
- Formal pension valuation
- Privately owned business paperwork
- Insurance policies and statements

Your lawyer should review your financial disclosure documents to ensure you have all the information needed and that you're happy with your knowledge of where your finances stand. Depending on where you live, financial disclosure by both parties is required by law. Common excuses for not wanting to provide disclosure — including "my spouse already knows my finances" or "this information is private" or "if my spouse sees real numbers, they will want more of my money" — are invalid.

Common Ways to Proceed With Divorce and Alternatives to Court

There are numerous ways that can be used to sort out the details of a divorce. The costs involved can vary vastly depending on which route a couple takes.

Judge

This is the route Divya and Ethan went, but it's not the most common route these days. If you're in a high-stress, acrimonious relationship or separation, and you're fully anticipating a contentious divorce, this will likely be what your lawyer suggests. If the separation isn't friendly and you can't deal with issues outside of the court system, going before a judge to decide the case is likely inevitable. "In my view, it's a last-ditch option," says Russell Alexander. "When you think about it, you're letting a third party decide when and where you see your children. Leaving it up to a stranger to decide what's right for your family isn't ideal. It's a terrible experience for people to go through." Court is also very expensive, it's often delayed (you might not get a date with a judge for many months, and it can even last years, depending on the situation) and a judge is not going to be able to fully appreciate your individual family dynamic with the limited amount of time they have to devote to each family before them.

Still, this might be the right decision for you if you and your spouse are unable to communicate and will have too much difficulty negotiating.

Collaborative Family Law

In this type of family law, there's a focus on goals and interests, and you tell your lawyer what's most important for you and your family. There's a focus on being non-adversarial; the guiding principle is respect and there's a pledge to settle out of court. Lawyers will then come up with an agreement based on what you tell them you want, not necessarily based on what the law says. Alexander says this is very effective for family-run businesses that are usually destroyed by divorce. "If spouses want the business to continue, we come up with creative options so it can survive after divorce." In this scenario, lawyers will agree to be civil, they agree not to go to court, and promise to provide all the information that's needed to settle. Other specialists may assist lawyers and participants such as a chartered professional accountant, chartered business valuator (CBV), certified financial planner® (CFP), family dispute resolution pactitioner (FDRP), social worker, etc. If this is the route you want to go, both parties hire their own collaborative family lawyer and there's clarity around expectations and needs, especially when it comes to any children. Alexander says he encourages going the collaborative route to ninety percent of his clients.

There's another plus when you choose to go this way: the team of experts you will work with to sort out difficult issues. Renée le Nobel is an accountant in Vancouver. She also works as a "financial neutral" with Collaborative Divorce Vancouver. She specializes in listening to her clients' financial situations in a "non-threatening and empathetic way." Le Nobel practices what she preaches, and she's no stranger to the subject matter — she understands the stress and financial issues that come from marital collapse because she went through a divorce herself. "I got into this work after my divorce. The collaborative process is designed to keep people out of the court system and keep the decision-making in the client's hands. If you go this route, you have a team to rely on, including mental health professionals, child specialists, and financial experts. Going through a separation and divorce is one of the most stressful things you can do in life. My role as a financial neutral is all about helping people get a clear sense of what their financial situation is now and what it will look like going forward. The collaborative process transitions people to a better life post-separation," she says. "Financial literacy — or a lack thereof — is real, and people come into this process having no idea what their financial situation is. I often see one spouse has a very good idea of family finances and one spouse doesn't; that's the usual dynamic and that's the nature of marriage. I help gather financial information, put it all into a spreadsheet and say, 'Here's your net worth,' and then help them put together a post-separation cash flow and say, 'Here's how much money you have (or don't have) to spend.' The simple step of helping separating spouses get on the same page regarding the family's financial situation allows them to have a far superior separation process and astronomically more successful lives post-separation. The more challenging step for me as a financial neutral is convincing potential clients to work with their spouse to do the financial information gathering instead of fighting with their spouse and letting the inefficient and costly court system do this step." Le Nobel tells me about one couple with whom she worked — the husband was the breadwinner, and the wife raised their kids as a stay-at-home parent. The husband got into financial difficulty and was embarrassed and ashamed, so he hid their financial issues. "Going through their finances, I could see the family was underwater. They were about $500,000 in debt and the wife had no idea. As far as she was concerned, her spouse was a professional with a good job. It's not easy to find out this kind of information, especially when you're going through a divorce. Luckily, the wife had retained a collaborative lawyer, which allowed us to design a separation process that worked for the family. So, we got them a separation agreement, and they now have a plan. The husband felt a sense of relief because he didn't have to hide anymore. It worked out well." One of the most common situations le Nobel sees are couples where one party doesn't pay attention to the family finances. "It's the nature of the family system. You divide and conquer and do what you're good at; one person doesn't pay attention, one person does. Mix that in with the stress of a separation, which is emotional, and the person who isn't involved with the family finances has an immediate distrust of what the other person is doing, even if their spouse was completely above board. If you have one neutral person gathering the numbers and doing the walk-throughs with the couple and their lawyer, you build trust, especially in contentious situations." Le Nobel is a fan of education, and she encourages people to find a licenced financial planner or another financial expert who has knowledge in providing financial advice during a divorce. "For some clients, this is the wake-up call they needed — a kick in the pants to get on top of their finances. Many people are looking at this kind of dispute resolution as opposed to going to court. The stories are true — a court process can cost hundreds of thousands, and that's money you could've used to put your kids through school or saved for your retirement."

The opportunity costs of getting divorced will have a compounding effect on the future of your finances. For example, let's say legal fees associated with a divorce cost $100,000, which could've otherwise been invested into a portfolio for your retirement. After 20 years, $100,000 in a portfolio that yields 5% per year would be worth $265,000 in pre-tax savings. The costs of not engaging the appropriate legal, financial, or mental health professional could have a significant adverse impact on the finances of you and your family in the future.

Mediation

This involves an impartial third party who helps the negotiations and works to settle your case. They are not at liberty to give legal advice or act as an advocate for either side — their job is simply to listen to what you want and to help you reach an agreement on any of property division, child support, spousal support, parenting arrangements, and any other issues. They do not make decisions for you, but they may make suggestions when there are particularly difficult issues. Lawyers can be present during mediation sessions. If there's an agreement as a result of mediation, the mediator will draft the settlement terms and have it edited by the parties and their lawyers. Like collaborative family law, mediation relies on a commitment to resolving the issues while respecting everyone's goals. It also relies on the exchange of information. You should always show your lawyer any agreement that's decided during mediation before you sign. Mediators generally charge an hourly rate, but the cost depends on whether you go to a private or a government-funded mediator, as well as your annual income. In Ontario, for example, the cost can be a nominal amount per hour and can go up to several hundreds of dollars per hour; please check your appropriate provincial/territorial resources (link available in the glossary/resources section).

Arbitration

This is another form of dispute resolution where an arbitrator (a paid third party) decides on an outcome in a similar way a judge would. Their decision is final and legally binding, and depending on their qualifications, can deal with issues such as division of property and equalization payments, child and/or spousal support, and parenting arrangements. If both spouses agree to arbitration, they sign an arbitration agreement that explains who will arbitrate, where and when it will take place, and the issues that will be included in arbitration. This is assuming that both parties agree on the division of assets, support payments, child custody, etc., and are essentially splitting everything down the middle. If you've tried mediation and you're at an impasse, an arbitrator can make a decision on your case.

Do-It-Yourself

This is not a recommended solution. Attempting to come up with your own DIY separation agreement might seem like a good idea, especially if there isn't bad blood between you and your spouse. It might also seem like the most cost-effective option, but beware — the risk of improperly preparing and executing a DIY separation agreement is high, which, in turn, could have severe, long-lasting financial impacts on you in the future. You really need a trained expert in preparing a separation agreement. Remember, your separation agreement is a legally-binding document that will cost even more to fix if it's not done properly.

Simple and Joint Divorces

In Canada, either partner can initiate divorce proceedings. The simple divorce means that one of the spouses has filed for an uncontested divorce, while the joint divorce means both spouses have filed for the divorce application together. In Ontario, for example, the simple divorce, as defined by the province, is filed when one of the parties isn't cooperating in signing the joint divorce application due to lack of communication or if the other spouse isn't cooperating when it comes to paying court and legal fees. The joint divorce is filed when both spouses are cooperative with one another and the lines of communication are open. Generally, the joint divorce application is processed faster than the simple divorce application.

The Amicable Divorce

This is definitely the cheaper option when it comes to divorce. If your divorce is amicable (or uncontested), not only will your legal fees most likely be lower, but it can also speed up the process in divorce proceedings. (Plus, it's much less emotionally draining than the contested divorce.) In an amicable divorce, both spouses agree on terms together (for example, parenting time, decision-making, and child support payments), and then a judge certifies the agreement (an administrative procedure). This settles the separation and divorce without needing to go to court.

The Contested Divorce

If you want to fight your ex-partner, be prepared to pay. Contested divorces happen when both parties can't come to an agreement about the terms of their divorce, including parenting schedules, child support, spousal support, allocation of debts, etc. This type of divorce is more complex and often quite contentious, so it takes longer (and it's the more emotionally draining of the two options). The cost for a contested divorce can vary vastly depending on where you live, the experience level and number of lawyers involved, and the complexity of the case.

Misconceptions about the Cost of Divorce

Jessica Chapman says cost really depends on the parties. "If you have two people who are on the same page who come to a resolution and are ready to be reasonable, where they're not wanting to take their partner for everything they're worth and who are ready to listen to a lawyer, I quote $1,500 for a separation agreement. If you have one or two parties who aren't going to be reasonable — and I see these types of clients all the time — people who aren't going to cooperate, in that case, where you do not agree on anything and you don't have a client who is able to choose their battles wisely, it can be very expensive. In some cases, more than six figures," she says. "The misconception around the cost is that it's going to be very expensive, period, but it really doesn't have to be. It really depends on the relationship between the parties. If you're able to reasonably discuss things with the other party, it doesn't have to be expensive. But ... [even] if you are the person being reasonable and [who] just wants to move on, you can't control the other person's reaction to the things that you propose and you can't control whether they're going to be reasonable or not."

The biggest piece of advice Chapman has for people going through a separation is to choose their battles wisely. "As you can probably guess, I've written letters to opposing counsel about even the most menial of things such as garden hostas — he dug them up and she wants them back. The cost of these plants is literally a fraction of the cost that it would take to pay me to write that letter, and it's those clients who can't see the forest through the trees who really end up racking up huge legal bills. Quite honestly, I can often tell in our very first call where this is going to go based on their reaction to some of the things I tell them about the law or based on whether they just went on a fifteen- to twenty-minute rant about how he didn't pay half the cost for the fifty-dollar registration for soccer. If that's what's coming up on our initial call, I know where this is headed and I will give them the spiel about choosing your battles and doing a constant cost-benefit analysis of what is worth fighting over, which I encourage clients to do with me throughout the entirety of their file," she explains. For example, if Chapman and a client are spending a lot of time discussing the car loan of $8,000 and the client has already spent $2,000 in legal fees discussing the loan, "maybe we should bite this bullet. I will tell clients candidly what I think is worth fighting over. If it's a half-million-dollar investment, of course, if you're entitled to half of that, you might need to spend some money if they're not going to fork it over. Sometimes it's basic math."

But sometimes it's not basic math. Sometimes when you're talking about parenting time and decision-making, it doesn't matter how much money it costs. "I've told clients that my best guess is that we're not going to be successful and that means you're going to spend X amount in legal fees and you could get dinged with costs after a hearing and

I've had clients say, 'I don't care, I need to try. I don't care how much this costs; for my own sanity, I need to try because I won't be satisfied otherwise.' For some clients when it comes to children, there is no cost-benefit analysis, it is always worth it for their kids. Despite this, I always discuss with them the impact that litigation can have on children, and the relationship with the other party, who they may have to co-parent with for many years."

How to Cut Costs

While many will be tempted to cut the costs associated with divorce, the decision on whether it makes sense to cut costs will be based on each individual person's own facts and circumstances. While cutting costs may sound like the prudent thing to do, in the long run the "costs" of only focusing on minimizing the costs might end up costing you significantly in the future if you don't structure the divorce appropriately. At a minimum, it's usually wise to seek proper legal advice when figuring out the best option based on everyone's own facts and circumstances. If cost minimization still make sense, the list below highlights some ideas to help:

1) As previously suggested, go the amicable/uncontested divorce route. This may still involve having a lawyer to review your agreement, but it's easier and cheaper overall.
2) Agree on everything you can. It might not be easy (it could be downright difficult), but try to agree on as much as you can with your ex-spouse. The more you agree on, the better, the cheaper, the easier you get it. If you go the mediation route, you will really lessen the amount you're going to spend by avoiding litigation. For example, in Quebec, free family mediation sessions are offered up to a fixed number of hours, depending on the situation. Quebecers receive a two-and-a-half-hour session on parenting after separation; five hours of mediation, if you're in the process of separating; and two-and-a-half hours of mediation, if you already have an agreement or court judgement but wish to have it reviewed, if you and your

ex-spouse have already received family mediation services, or if you have already obtained a judgement ordering a legal separation. The Ministère de la Justice pays the fees.

3) Check to see if you qualify for legal aid. In a contested divorce, low-income people may be eligible for free or inexpensive legal counsel provided by legal aid.

4) Consider using a collaborative family lawyer. In this process, you and your former partner (with your respective lawyers) must sign an agreement that says the lawyers will drop your case if the four of you don't negotiate and reach a settlement.

5) Get a good grasp on your finances. Create a budget and sit down with trusted licenced financial adviser (e.g. chartered professional accountant, certified financial planner, etc.) to understand your finances moving forward. This is a new stage in life and it will help you in the long run if you have a good idea of where you are financially now and where you'd like to be in the future.

6) Be mindful of your interactions with your lawyer. There's no denying you need someone in your corner to work with you through the legal aspects of the divorce, but remember that each interaction with your lawyer adds up. Each time your lawyer sends an email or picks up the phone, you're being billed. It's a good idea to write down any questions prior to communications so you don't waste time during the conversation. If you need additional emotional support through the process, your money is better spent on a therapist or psychologist who can help you address those issues.

7) Get your documents ready and be prepared. This can amount to huge savings in the end. You don't want to be searching for paperwork or unsure of specific dates when you go for your consultation with your lawyer. Make a list of all the dates you'll be asked about — the date of your marriage, date of separation, when you started living with your ex-spouse, children's birthdates, etc. You should also come armed with documents that might help your lawyer sort out your financial situation, including your last three years of tax returns, bank account statements, credit card

statements, loan documents, mortgage statements, marriage contract or prenuptial agreement (if you have one), insurance statements, etc.

Bringing in a Licenced Financial Professional

For Chapman, there are two main reasons lawyers bring in a licenced financial professional who specialize in family-law matters:

1) for the calculation of the valuation of a business ("valuing a business is a nuanced exercise and having an expert value the business is a big deal," she says); and
2) to complete what she calls a guideline income report.

"[Guideline income reports] are done when we have a person who would be required to pay either child or spousal support and they're self-employed and determining their income for the purposes of child or spousal support is difficult — it can be very nuanced, so we get an accountant to do this report. The accountant looks over all of the business financials, income tax returns, notices of assessment for both the corporation and the person and often they'll meet with the person whose income is being determined and ask them a plethora of questions. Then they do their report based on their analysis and will present the amount they believe the income should be for the purposes of child or spousal support," she says.

It's also helpful to bring in accountants to discuss the tax side — who will claim tax deductions or credits relating to your dependents or claim child benefits (such as the Canada Child Benefit). Or how splitting assets will occur — transfers from RRSPs to another RRSP generally have no immediate tax consequences, but sometimes the agreement is worded that the transferor can choose whether to use RRSP funds or non-registered funds, and that impacts the after-tax value for the recipient.

Raj and Christine went through with the divorce. In the end, they opted for a collaborative lawyer and worked with each other to decide the best arrangement for their family. "I was really worried about what life would look like on one income, but I met with my accountant several times and she helped me come up with a plan that works for me. I have a customized spreadsheet where I list everything that comes in and goes out, and I find that keeps me on top of my finances. The challenge is taking the time to fill out the spreadsheet, but because it's taught me a lot about how I spend and save money, it's worth it."

CHAPTER TWO

The Big Picture

AMELIA MET HER EX, CARL, in South America. They were both on vacation and it turned out they were from neighbouring cities — even had a few favourite haunts in common. They hit it off and after two weeks away, the new couple decided to continue their romance when they returned home.

After a good five years together — and both in their mid-thirties — they ultimately decided it was time to get married. Amelia says it wasn't a big deal for either of them to make things official, and they decided to go for it.

Carl and Amelia were married for ten years. "We were mostly happy, until we weren't," Amelia says. "I ended it. There were a variety of reasons why — including I felt like I had a business partner instead of a husband — but one of the bigger reasons was money. He was terrible with it and I wore the pants when it came to making it." She found a paralegal to keep the cost of the divorce down. It's important to note that paralegals are not licenced to practice family law in all provinces. Check with your local licensing authority to determine if this option is available to you.

The couple had no marriage contract, but because they were amicable, Amelia decided to help Carl. "I took over the lease on the car, we sold the house and split it fifty-fifty, I paid off the debt on the line of credit and when we both walked away, we had $40,000 from the house sale. Well, he blew through that in a year. His parents live in Europe and he wanted to go visit them and didn't even have the money to do that, so I loaned him $5,000. He's never paid it back," she says. "We also share our two dogs and he's always told me he'd pay half of their care and vet bills, but I haven't seen that either."

There are a lot of predictable issues that come out of separation and divorce. These are the things you've probably already been thinking about, like what to do with your family home, how assets are divided, and how debt you accumulated throughout your marriage works — what you are on the hook for and what your ex is going to have to deal with. The truth is, these are big issues, and the good news is, once you understand how it all works, it's not too difficult to figure out. What you might not know is how these things will affect your overall financial picture.

Equalization and Dividing Property

Depending on which province or territory you live in, the value of the property you acquire during your marriage must be shared equally when you divorce. The value of a property is attributed to one spouse or other based on how title is held or who it belongs to (for instance if an item was gifted from one spouse to the other). For example, in Ontario, the value of the family home, car, pension, money, furniture, and business (if applicable) will be tallied for each spouse in the equalization process. Any property you owned prior to getting married is counted too — if that property increased in value during the marriage, then the increase in value is included in the equalization calculation. Please check your appropriate provincial/territorial resources (link available in the glossary/resources section) for specifics in your case.

A matrimonial home that was purchased prior to marriage is treated differently. Even if it was bought prior to the marriage, if the matrimonial home is still owned on the date of separation, you will have to share the full value with your ex-spouse, unless you have excluded it in a marriage contract. (More on that in "The Matrimonial Home.")

Dividing property is generally done in the separation agreement. Both parties should have their own lawyer look over the agreement before you sign. While it is not necessary to immediately rush into negotiations when it becomes clear that your relationship is over, it is important to keep in mind that there are time limits associated with certain legal claims. In Ontario, for instance, you have six years from the day you separated or two years from the day your divorce is final to go to court for a decision on the amount of an equalization payment.

There are exceptions that will allow one spouse to avoid equalizing the value of certain assets (called "excluded property"). Examples include inheritances or gifts from someone other than your spouse while you were married; money you received from an insurance company because someone died; money you received or have a right to as a result of a personal injury (such as a car accident); and property you or your spouse have agreed to exclude through an agreement.

If your family home is on a big property that's used for other purposes, only the house and the area around it are considered the family home. This means that if your home is, say, on a farm, the entire farm isn't considered the family home. Courts may divide property differently in unique and special situations. Your lawyer can explain whether these exceptions apply to your situation.

If you have a marriage contract, you could be looking at a different scenario. Marriage contracts are legally binding documents couples sign before they get married to protect their rights (including rights related to property) in the event they eventually decide to end their marriage. These contracts can incorporate specific details such as how you'll divide your property; and how much spousal support each party will pay. (They do not include parenting time with children or decision-making responsibilities when it comes to kids.) You should never sign a marriage contract without independent legal advice. Marriage contracts should be looked over by separate lawyers for both parties prior to signing. These contracts can decrease the amount of conflict a couple experiences following a separation, but there are specific things that courts will look for when determining whether a marriage contract is valid, including but not limited to whether both parties had independent legal advice and whether full financial disclosure was made. As a family's circumstances change, changes can be made to marriage contracts if they're made in writing and signed in front of a witness. If after you separate, you don't agree with the terms of your contract, you'll need to go before a judge to ask for a decision to be made if you and your ex-spouse can't agree about changing the terms.

The total of each spouse's net worth that accrued during the marriage is called their net family property. The process of determining which spouse has a lower net family property and is therefore entitled to an equalization payment is called the equalization of net family properties. The payment owed as a result of the equalization of net family properties is the equalization payment.

When it comes to what you're owed, adding up the value of your property and dividing it between you and your spouse can be contentious. Your best bet is to consult a lawyer as there may be various exceptions that apply to your situation. At a high level, to figure out what you owe or are owed, you start by adding up the value of all the property you owned as of the day you separated and deduct the value of your debts and excluded property as of the same date. In this case, property may include homes, furniture, cars, businesses, jewellery, bank savings, and investment accounts (including Registered Retirement Savings Plans, Tax-Free Savings Accounts, Registered Education Savings Plans, and pensions). Your debts may include your mortgage, money owned on credit cards, and car loans.

After you add up your property at the date of separation, do the same for the day you got married, except for any debts (i.e. mortgage or line of credit) that were owed for the family home on the date of marriage, if applicable. Calculate the difference and you get your net family property. If it's a negative number, it's considered to be zero. Then, do the same to determine your spouse's net family property. Compare the value of your net family property to the value of your spouse's net family property. The spouse with the larger net family property must make an equalization payment to the spouse with the smaller net family property. The equalization payment is equal to one-half of the difference between your respective net family properties.

So, for example, if one spouse is worth $17,000 and the other is worth $2,000, the difference between the two is $15,000 and the spouse with the higher net family property will need to make an equalization payment of $7,500 so that both spouses end up with a net worth of $9,500.

Of course, there are exceptions to this rule. If the spouses have a marriage contract that specifies how their assets are divided if they divorce, the marriage contract should be followed. Other exceptions include when one spouse depletes their property to avoid paying the other spouse an equalization payment; when one spouse incurs a lot of debts and those debts are now reducing the amount of their property; and if they live together for less than five years and if an equalization payment were done, one spouse would receive a much larger payment.

Kelly LaVallie, a Vancouver-based chartered professional accountant and certified divorce financial analyst says, "That philosophical statement 'my ex and I want to be fair with one another so we're doing this ourselves' makes me break into a cold sweat for those people. Because what does that even mean? And how do you know it means the same thing to your ex that it means to you? To me, divorce is a legal and business transaction and there's family law that defines each person's best- and worst-case scenario. For example, if women stayed home and raised the kids while their husband went out and worked, but had no entitlement for spousal support under the law, then in his opinion, perhaps it would be fair not to pay spousal support. I really feel like fair is so subjective that it's somewhat irrelevant and what matters is what's the law and then within the law there's a range. I think being fair is almost kind of a red herring — I think you each need to know the law and hopefully neither of you get entrenched because of your emotions and hopefully you can stay reasonable. I think maybe that's a better goal than fair."

Example: George and Maria (From Ontario's Ministry of the Attorney General); please visit your provincial/territorial Attorney General website for specific resources. Visit the glossary/resources section of this publication for direct links.

STEPS	George	Maria	
Step 1: Find the value of the property you had on the day you separated	$ 47,000	$ 12,000	A
Step 2: Subtract the value of the debts you owed on the day you separated	$ (8,000)	$ (2,000)	B
Step 3: Subtract the value of the property that the law allows you to keep for yourself	$ (4,000)		C
Step 4: Subtract the value of your property at the time of marriage, less the value of debts	$ (18,000)	$ (8,000)	D
Step 5: Total value of family property	**$ 17,000**	**$ 2,000**	**$ E = A – B – C – D**
The equalization payment is calculated as the difference between in the total value of family of the two spouses divided by 2.			
Now do the math			
Total value of family property attributable to George	$ 17,000		
Less: total value of family property attributable to Maria	$ (2,000)		
	$ 15,000		
Divide by:	2		
Total equalization payment to be made by George	**$ 7,500**		

George has to make an equalization payment of $7,500 to Maria so they are each left with the same amount, $9,500.

Common Questions About Dividing Property (From Ontario's Ministry of the Attorney General)

Q: I'm entitled to a payment of $10,000. Do I get this in cash?

A: Possibly. The payment can be made in cash, but it can also be made by giving you property worth $10,000. The way you'll be paid out can be arranged in your separation agreement, or the court can decide.

Q: Can our separation agreement divide things differently than from the way the law says?

A: Yes, you can divide your property in any way that works for you in your separation agreement. Both your lawyer and your ex-spouse's lawyer should look over the separation agreement before either of you sign it. It's very difficult to change your separation agreement later, so ensure this step is completed.

Q: I got a car as a gift from my parents. The law says that I don't have to share the value of gifts I received during my marriage with my ex-spouse. I've decided to sell the car. Once I sell, is the money I get for it part of the property I must share with my ex?

A: It depends what you do with that money. If you keep it separate, for example, in a savings bond so that it can always be traced back to the sale of the car, it will be excluded from the property you have to share when your marriage ends. The exception to this rule is about the family home. If you use the money from the sale of the car to pay down the mortgage on your matrimonial home or if you renovate it, you must share the full value of the family home with your ex-spouse. Once the money is put into the family home, it must be shared, even if it came from a gift or inheritance.

Q: My husband has been paying into company pension plans for thirty years. I stayed home and raised the kids. We separated. Do I have a right to share his pension?

A: Yes, pension is included in the calculation of your spouse's share of the family property at separation. If you're owed an equalization payment, you can agree to or ask the court for an order for all or part of the payment that is owed to you to be made from the pension.

Q: My parents left me their house when they died, and I've been living in it for two years with my boyfriend. We want to get married. If our marriage doesn't work out, I don't want to lose the house to him. Can I say the house is mine in our marriage contract?

A: Yes, your marriage contract can absolutely say that you own the house and that its value when you married and any increase in its value during your marriage is yours. If you decide to separate, your spouse won't have financial claim to your house, but they will have the same right as you to stay in the family home. You can't put anything in writing to change this.

Q: We live on a big dairy farm. Is the whole farm considered our family home?

A: No, your family home is the part of the farm where you live — the house and the small area around the house. The rest is property like any other property.

Q: I can't deal with making lists of property right now. How much time do I have?

A: You have six years from the day you separated to go to court to ask for a decision on equalization payments. If you've already divorced, you have two years from the date the divorce is final.

Q: I moved out and I'm worried my ex will get rid of our family property just so he doesn't have to share its value with me. What can I do?

A: You can go to court and ask a judge to stop him from giving away the property. The court can tell him not to sell or dispose of the property, or order it be put in someone else's care.

Q: We're common law and have been living together for fifteen years. Do we have to share the value of our property?

A: It's possible. Married couples have a legal right to half the value of family property, but you can go to court to make your claim. You should ask a lawyer for advice.

Common-Law Couples

These couples aren't legally required to split property acquired during the time they lived together. This means that household items, furniture, and any other property belongs to the person who bought them. Common-law couples don't have the right to split an increase in value of the property they brought into the relationship.

If you're a common law couple in British Columbia and New Brunswick, for example, any household belongings and other property belong to the person who brought them into the relationship. These couples don't have the same rights as married couples — they aren't required to split the increase in value of the property they brought with them. That said, if you've contributed to property your spouse owns, you could have a right to part of it. You will have to go to court to get your contribution back unless your partner agrees to pay you.

When it comes to these bigger issues, LaVallie says if there's any complexity at all, an accountant should be involved. "Accountants can help you identify assets that are going to create challenges. They can see possible problems that might be caused by dividing up assets and debts, as well as issues that have big future tax implications, such as RRSPs. With their help, you start to see the roadmap of the handful of issues that are going to be challenging. I help my clients and their lawyers come up with strategies of how we might tackle those issues," she explains. She says accountants will review all financial information (including personal and corporate tax returns) and help educate the lawyer and client on overall net worth, income, expenses and financial issues that will need to be dealt with. "It's pretty common that people don't have a sense of their financial big picture. My goal is to help the lawyer and my client understand this picture." She also reminds clients that between separating and getting their separation agreement finalized, ex-spouses are still very much financially connected. "This is a big challenge, too — how you deal with what I call the 'limbo period' between separating and getting your deal done is something many people don't think about."

Misconceptions About Separation and Splitting Assets

1) The separation date doesn't matter. "Many people think everything is valued when they get around to doing it or when they finally decide to go to a lawyer. But contacting a lawyer isn't usually the first thing you do when you separate — it takes you time. We often see people, especially in collaborative family law, where they're figuring things out and sometimes, we don't see people until a couple of months after they've separated. I think people are surprised that you have to go back to that date three or four months ago when you actually separated when we're valuing your assets and debts, unless both spouses agree to use a different date for valuation," says Robynne Kazina, a partner at Taylor McCaffrey LLP in Winnipeg.

2) Separation doesn't necessarily mean being physically apart. "I think people are surprised about a 'legal' separation — people think you have to be physically separated to be separated, but you don't. You can live in the same house and still be separated. People also think you need a legal separation agreement to be considered separated, but that's not true either. I think there's a lot of misunderstanding about what does it mean to be separated. It just means one person decides they want to separate. It doesn't have to be a mutual agreement. When there's a disagreement about separation date, case law looks at when you told your friends and family, whether you slept in separate bedrooms, when you stopped eating meals together — the actual day-to-day circumstances that would point to whether you're really still a couple or not," says Kazina. (In other words, even if you're still living together for the kids or for other reasons, you must live as if you're separated — carrying on as if you're still together and acting as a couple could signal to others that you're still in a relationship.)

There can be several misconceptions around separation and its impact when splitting assets. The important thing to do is seek proper legal advice to help you understand the many factors to consider when going through a divorce.

DIVIDING ASSETS WITH ROBYNNE KAZINA, A PARTNER AT TAYLOR McCAFFRETY LLP IN WINNIPEG

Kazina says the law is different in each province when it comes to how the division of family property works. In Manitoba, for example, you essentially share fifty percent (subject to certain exclusions) of whatever you own at the date of separation. There are two key pieces of information you need to know to properly divide assets.

1) The importance of an actual date of separation. "You can't just say, 'we separated in January.' We need an actual date.

Legally, it's on that date that accounting is completed that we look at the value of all assets and debts," she explains.

2) The importance of fair market value. "So, this is how much a third party would buy it from you. Like your car, for example — how much could a third party buy the car for; how much could you sell it for? It's not how much did you pay for it, how much do you want for it, how much is it to replace. It's fair market value. The same goes for your house. How much could you sell it for? That's the test. For example, if the average price you can sell your car for is $20,000, the fair market value of your car is $20,000, regardless of whether you paid $40,000 for the car three years ago."

Dividing Household Contents

Q: My mother passed down my grandmother's china set — she received it as a gift when she got married. Is the set now my husband's because we're married? What happens to it when we get divorced?

A: The china set is still your property in the event of divorce. However, if it's increased in value since you got married, you and your spouse will share the increase in value. If you have a marriage contract, you could've had the china written in — it could say it's your property and that any increase in its value during your marriage won't be shared if the marriage ends. If this isn't the case, you split the increase in value.

Yes, this is where Aunt Bertha's hutch, your televisions, and dishes come into play. For the most part, the experts are all on the same page when it comes to these items: Don't sweat the small stuff. The money and time you spend fighting over this stuff will probably be worth more than the actual item you're bickering about. (What's more, if you can navigate this part of your separation without your lawyer, you'll certainly save a few bucks.) Kazina says that many family lawyers and family court judges sometimes get frustrated when people want to value their household contents. The reason people get caught up in this exercise is because many of their household bits and pieces have a strong sentimental value. "People often have a strong emotional connection to their things, even though on the financial side, it's not really that significant because how much something is worth is essentially how much you'd sell it for at a garage sale. For example, a piano. Even though you purchased the piano, and they can be very expensive, they're hard to sell. There are a lot of things that have a lot of sentimental value, but when it comes down to putting a price tag on it, it comes down to how much you could sell it for basically on Kijiji," she says. What most people do and what most lawyers recommend for division of household assets is you and your spouse come up with a list that you feel is equitable — one spouse keeps all these items, the other keeps all these items, and without putting a dollar on each item, you get to a point where you feel your list is fair and equitable. "That's the way many people will deal with their household contents. Unless there's a significant art collection, for example, there are not really any household contents for which they shouldn't be able to come up with a fair split." When it comes to your children's possessions (toys, etc.), you've likely already given them the responsibility to keep their toys in good condition, to put them away after use, etc. Many experts suggest it's a good idea to continue to allow your child make the call when it comes to their things: Will their stuffed-animal collection stay at Dad's house, or does the child want to split it and bring their teddy bears to Mom's house? Your best bet is to give children (who are old enough to understand what's happening) the space and responsibility to decide. This could give them some power back and help them get through these difficult times.

The Matrimonial or Family Home

It depends on where you live across Canada, but the matrimonial home is often treated differently from other assets due to the nature of the relationship that families have with their home — even if one person bought the home prior to the marriage, it is often the case that the other partner would have eventually contributed money toward the maintenance and upkeep of the home or toward the mortgage or utility bills. The matrimonial home almost always belongs to both spouses, even if one purchased before marriage, or only one name is on the title. These are just some of the reasons that the value of the family home is divided between spouses when they separate or divorce. In most cases, the home is sold, either to one of the spouses or to a third-party buyer. Details of this should be in your separation agreement. Lawyer Jessica Chapman says property division when married varies province to province, but in Nova Scotia — regardless of whose name an asset is in, both parties are entitled to half its value, if it's a matrimonial asset — it's an equal division of all assets regardless of when you acquired them, even if it was before the marriage. When it comes to the family home, there's often back and forth about who contributed what. In Nova Scotia, it doesn't matter if one person owned it before or if it was just bought with one person's money and it doesn't even matter whose name is on the house. However, there are a list of circumstances where the court will consider an unequal division of assets and one of those is the duration of the marriage," she says.

Here's the thing about the matrimonial house: it's tied to a ton of emotions. "In those early days when you're separated, your entire life is turned on its ear. So much changes and you don't have a clear sense yet of what your financial life is going to look like when the dust settles. Everything is up in the air — change, fear, uncertainty — and you're trying to decide what to do with the family home. I think that's a bit of a challenging recipe because we can only tolerate so much change and some may be inclined to keep the family home, even in a circumstance where it doesn't make sense," says accountant LaVallie. "I encourage clients to defer these big, more permanent-type questions. Making that decision before you have a sense of what your post-divorce life is going to look like is a risky thing to do. In the early days, you probably don't have a clear sense of what your financial obligation will look like, whether you're the payer or the receiver [recipient], and you maybe don't have a clear sense of what your employment will look like either. The idea of what you can afford and the way your life might change, you need to explore, get pragmatic, if possible, even though it's an emotional topic. You want to remember that you're buying your partner out or they're buying you out when the deal is done, so you want to think about things like whether the market is high or low. Think about the state of the market and where it's going, your capacity to keep the home and not just from a financial perspective, you also have to maintain it. Is it the right place for you?"

Do You Buy Out Your Spouse or Sell and Split the Proceeds?

There are tons of reasons for wanting to stay in the family home. This is the place where your kids feel stable. You might love your neighbours and neighbourhood amenities, or you might just really love your home, after years of putting so much into it. This is all understandable. But when it comes down to it, the experts all agree that deciding whether to sell or to buy out your spouse and stay in the home is ultimately about money. The experts also agree that you're going to need to consider several things when you're deciding what works best for you:

- Do you only want to keep the house because you're worried about your kids' stability? Children are more resilient than you think. Don't make a huge financial commitment based on guilt around your kids.
- Would you rather stay in this house, with all the past memories of your ex, or make a new life for yourself in a new home?
- If you take on the house and buy out your ex, will you end up being house poor? Can you afford the mortgage on your own? Is this a financial expense you think you should take if you're considering your future?
- Can you take care of the house on your own? If your ex was the one who handled snow removal and lawn maintenance and house repairs, for example, will you be able to do these things by yourself or have the financial capacity to pay someone to do them?

If you're considering keeping your house because you've seen how much the house has gone up in value, try not to think about what's happened in the past, advises LaVallie. You don't know what's going to happen with the housing market in your area and you should be cautious about relying on the past. "For example, if your house has gone up three percent every year for fifteen years, that's a good sign it will continue to go up, but you don't know what will happen going forward, so you can't bank on what's happened in the past."

Chapman says one of the most common misconceptions when it comes to deciding what to do with the house is the kind of value properties have. "There are often disagreements about the value of the home, but also, there are things to take into account when it comes to the home — there's the outstanding mortgage, the disposition costs (including a five percent real estate commission), the moving costs, the legal fees and HST on top of that," she says. "If you want to keep it and buy out your ex-spouse, you have to be able to keep the mortgage in your name alone. The bank has to be okay with you being the only one on the mortgage and for some people, that's just not possible," she explains.

Let's expand on this: a mortgage, like any other loan, is an obligation that needs to be paid back. From a lender's perspective, they'll require the existing borrowers to deal with the existing mortgage that's under the name of both spouses. This is because, as long as your name is on the mortgage, you're still liable for the mortgage even if you don't live there anymore. If your name stays on the mortgage, this will most likely impact your ability to borrow in the future. Generally, the spouse who no longer lives in the home will take their name off the mortgage.

The next issue that comes up relates to qualifying for a mortgage in the future and the amount of spousal and/or child support. Spousal and child support are included in the separation agreement. You will need a finalized separation agreement before you go your lender.

If you are the spouse paying spousal and/or child support, the lender looks at these payments as liabilities, and this will limit how much you can borrow on your next mortgage.

However, if you are the spouse receiving support payments the lender will allow you to include this as income, and when combined with employment income, this increases the amount available for you to borrow. However, it is important to note that support income when you are trying to qualify for a mortgage is usually not supposed to exceed one-third of your total household income, if it does, it will limit the amount you're able to borrow.

Common Questions Asked About Separation, Divorce, and the Family Home

Q: I bought the house before he moved in. My name is on the title. Doesn't that make the house my property?

A: Yes and no. The house belongs to you from a legal perspective. However, once a house that is owned by only one partner becomes a matrimonial home, in the absence of a marriage contract stating otherwise you are obligated to share the full value of the home with your partner if the marriage breaks down.

Q: We've separated and I moved out. Am I still responsible for the mortgage?

A: Yes, you are. If your name is on the mortgage, it's still your responsibility. In some instances, you may even be expected to continue making payments if your name is *not* on the mortgage but you have historically contributed to the mortgage payments in order to maintain the financial status quo pending an agreement with your ex-spouse.

Q: We have our house, but we also have a cottage. Are both considered matrimonial or family homes?

A: Most likely yes, they're both matrimonial homes. It is possible to have more than one matrimonial home. However, the term "matrimonial home" has a specific definition under provincial legislation so it is important to speak with a lawyer if you have questions about whether a specific property qualifies.

Q: My ex and I were common law. Do we split the home when we separate?

A: No, not necessarily. Common-law couples don't have the same rights when it comes to the matrimonial home. It depends whose name is on the title. You should speak to your lawyer.

Q: My ex moved out of our house when we separated. Does he still have a right to be in the house?

A: Yes, both spouses have a right to possession of (i.e. to stay in) the family home. In some cases, you can apply to a court for an order for exclusive possession. This will force your ex-spouse to live somewhere else. That said, it doesn't affect their ownership rights.

Buying Out Your Ex-spouse after Separation or Divorce

To do this, you'll need to take on the existing mortgage and pay out your ex-spouse's half of the equity you've made in the house. Most people going this route need to increase their mortgage to include the amount of money you'll owe your ex-spouse. For example, if your house is worth $1 million and you have a mortgage on the home for $500,000, that means the equity would be $500,000. Your ex-spouse would get half of that — $250,000. So, you'll have to take on the existing $500,000 mortgage and add another $250,000 to pay out your ex. Your new mortgage will be $750,000.

Valuing the Matrimonial Home

If you or your ex are buying the family home from the other, the value of the home is usually based on an appraisal done by a certified home appraiser. If you're selling to a third-party buyer, the value is the amount you can sell your home for.

"The matrimonial home is given special treatment upon separation and in any family law textbook you look at, you'll see a separate section on the matrimonial home. If it is registered in one person's name legally for real estate purposes, it stays registered in that person's name — they're still the legal owner, but any money that either spouse has put into it should be considered a gift to be shared with the other spouse. That is one of the big cautions that people need to know before they get married. Don't put a gift from a third party (like your parents) or an inheritance into that house if you do not genuinely want to share with your spouse. You cannot expect that your spouse will later agree that those funds should be returned to you if the house is sold or there is a separation. We often see parents buying their children a home as a wedding present. This can be a mistake, because the moment they do that, the money invested loses the protection it would otherwise have if it was not invested in the matrimonial home. It is possible to enter into a marriage contract before a marriage to protect the investment, but you cannot contract out of this as it is the law that provides a possessory right to matrimonial homes, which means that both spouses have the right to live there for a period of time post-separation. If the non-owning spouse wishes to, they could draw out the process so they can continue to stay in the home for an extended period, even years. It is really difficult to remove someone who is acting lawfully, and especially if there are children. It can get pretty tangled. Spouses can, in a marriage contract, waive their possessory right to stay in the home after a separation, but that waiver is not legally binding. They can change their mind when the separation occurs and the family court may take the waiver into consideration, but it is not a guarantee that the non-owning spouse will be removed. A married spouse cannot sell the property without the non-titled spouse's consent. There are so many complications and considerations around matrimonial homes. I frequently deal with separation cases in which a matrimonial home must be dealt with in a way one or both parties do not expect.

The need for marriage contracts or cohabitation agreements before marriage is increasing significantly because people are waiting now to get married until they actually have a career and assets — fewer people are getting married at nineteen when all they have is a milk crate and a motorbike. It's a completely different world now, so it's important to think your way through what each spouse wants and intends to have happen with their property and how much you want to share because the value of assets like the house or other gifts and inheritances that are comingled into family property are going to be considered marital property and subject to equalization (what we call division of marital property in Ontario) if you're not careful."

Debt and Divorce

According to Credit Canada, clients come to them with a handful of common questions about divorce and debt. While every divorce and debt situation is different, these questions and answers should be able to give you general information you can then confirm with your legal adviser or accountant.

Common Questions about Debt and Divorce

Q: **Am I on the hook for my ex's debt?**

A: You will likely have split your debts before the divorce and made arrangements to pay off what you owe individually. If not, debt resolution will be up to the court. Credit Canada says that from a lender's or creditor's perspective, "It doesn't matter. The person who borrowed the money is the person responsible for paying the debt. Even if the debt is under one spouse's name, but the other spouse spent the funds, it doesn't matter to the creditor. The person's name on the account is the person responsible for paying back the debt."

Q: **Can individual debts be shared in a divorce?**

A: Yes, but as stated, it doesn't matter to the lender or creditor. According to them, the person who borrowed the money is the responsible party.

Q: **What happens to joint credit cards in a divorce?**

A: "For joint credit card accounts, the best thing to do is to contact the lender to freeze the account so no more charges can go through — only payments will be accepted. Keep up with minimum payments until the courts can address repayment of the debt. You could also pay off the entire debt or transfer the balance to a new account in your name alone. But remember, the lender will hold you 100 percent responsible and it may have an impact on court proceedings," says Credit Canada. Seeking legal advice is probably your best bet here. This applies to supplementary cards as well!

Q: **What if debt you never knew existed is discovered — are you responsible?**

A: Credit Canada suggests pulling your credit report from Equifax or

TransUnion and sharing it with your former spouse. "Financial transparency is not only important during a marriage but also during a divorce. This way, there are no secrets, and you won't be caught off guard by undisclosed debt when things are being finalized. If one or neither partner wants to do this, things will eventually shake out, but it can get messy," it says.

What Do You Do if You're Worried Your Ex Is Hiding Money or Debt?

"If you're going through a divorce and you feel like you don't have the big picture, you're not sure about your family assets, and you're worried your ex is hiding something, know you're not alone. Many people in your situation have those fears," says LaVallie. It's very common to wonder if you have all of the information you need, so how do you know if something is missing? "This challenge is why you need an accountant. It's not even the goal to have every shred of information, but you need to have enough information to make an informed decision. I think people end up in two camps: One just has a number in mind with no information and if they get that number, they're happy. And the other end of the spectrum are the people who say, 'I cannot accept any deal until I know every transaction the family has had over the last fifteen years and I'm comfortable with it.' I don't subscribe to either of those camps. I recommend a middle ground. How do you decide on your bottom line when you're not informed? If you don't have the information, I just don't think it's responsible to name your bottom line. On the other hand, hiring a forensic accountant, spending years of your life and hundreds of thousands of dollars tracking down every last cent isn't the way to go either. Rely on your experts to get a relatively complete picture, a sense of the total assets and a decent idea of what they're all worth," she explains.

Back to Carl and Amelia. Regardless of their continuing financial issues (Carl still hasn't paid Amelia back for his trip abroad to see family), the two are still friendly with each other — as friendly as exes can be — and Amelia credits their relationship to her patience and good nature. When it comes to words of advice, she says she wishes she'd swallowed her pride during the relationship and held her tongue here and there, but she's quick to mention it takes both people to end a relationship and maintain a different kind of relationship after divorce. She also reinforces how impressed she was with the paralegal she went to — he was well-versed in all things divorce law, he was a good listener (and took the time to really understand what she wanted) and he was less expensive than going the typical lawyer route, which ultimately saved Amelia money. Remember, however, that paralegals are not licenced to practice family law in all provinces. Check with your local licencing authority to determine if this option is available to you.

CHAPTER THREE

The Nitty-Gritty

DARLA AND BRYAN WERE MARRIED for six years. They had one child together, who's now a teenager. It took four years to settle their divorce from the time of their separation. "We began dating when we were sixteen, we lived together, and worked together shortly after. I helped him through school. We owned a home together," she says.

"When we separated, we both got our own lawyers. It was so expensive; I had to borrow a lot of money from my grandmother. But there was no way of mediating — my ex is very aggressive and argumentative and there would've been no way to deal with him. Even with the lawyer, I ended up being way too easy on him and bent a lot on the settlements my lawyer attained. Honestly, I was fear-driven back then. I was afraid of losing Chloe, our daughter. I did nothing to warrant losing her, but that fear was crippling.

"I would do things one hundred percent differently now. It was really hard to make decisions regarding my life when I was at my lowest point. I was heartbroken and emotions were so high; it was difficult. I'm not even fully sure why the marriage ended. I feel he met someone else, although he denies it. I have phone records, stories from Chloe, and other things to back up my suspicions, but, you know, we won't go there. Let's just say he ended up getting married to the woman I had suspicions about. Maybe we just grew apart and no longer fit. He was negative and angry. That got tiring.

"I was always in charge of money because he was terrible at making payments on time. When we separated, he ran up our lines of credit and credit cards. I always had my own credit card as well, but I went out and got my own line of credit at that time, and then put holds on everything so he could not screw us any longer. He had no records of anything, so he had to request everything for his lawyers. On the other hand, I had every bank statement, credit card bill, and regular bill since the dawn of time. I went back through every ATM and debit transaction and researched who did what. It took hours and hours. My lawyer said he had never seen anything like it. Bryan's lawyer would start to argue something about spending and my lawyer would just laugh and pull out the proof.

"He stopped giving me money when we separated. He also conveniently got laid off. I went three months with all the household and child expenses on my plate with no help from him. I was making thirteen dollars an hour at the time. I lived on soup, turned every light off, unplugged everything. I laid blankets on the floor to save on heat. It was crazy. I got an emergency meeting with the judge, and he forced him to pay. However, since he had been 'laid off,' he had no money. I know he was getting paid under the table.

"He ended up using different lawyers throughout the process. The last one he got was at a huge discount because of his lack of income, and the guy was very disrespectful. He didn't feel like I deserved spousal support. I ended up being awarded just over $500 a month in child support, a few hundred in spousal support, and a good sum in money owed back, plus interest, from him running up the bills and household expenses, as well as court fees. The judge was good to me, and it could have been because my ex didn't show up to court a few times, he withheld paperwork, and made me pay more in legal fees by repeatedly not responding to emails or wanting words changed in documents.

"I was afraid of him and I caved. I dropped the spousal support and we settled on the list rate for his non-working income, which was $287 a month for child support. I did still take a good chunk owing that was allotted for expenses, but not the full amount. My poor lawyer would get so mad at me. He would work so hard to get me things and I would get scared and back off. To this day he is still only paying $287 a month because I never went back to the courts to get it increased. He makes good money today.

"As part of our court settlement, we put the house up for sale but it never sold. I learned he was filing for bankruptcy, so I had to as well or I would have been responsible for a lot of his debts. The house ended up having major problems that were too expensive to fix and no one would buy it. I was devastated. All my life I had never missed a bill or payment. I had a perfect credit rating, worked at a bank, etc. and now I had to file for bankruptcy. The house went back to the bank, and I moved in with my parents."

WE'VE COVERED THE BIG-PICTURE items and now it's time to look at the nitty-gritty — the finer details that, if you're like most people, you didn't even know you needed to deal with. These are the issues that don't necessarily jump out at you, like this question Raj (back in Chapter One) asked: you have "My credit is good. How do I protect it?" (The answer, by the way, is: You have to make sure you separate your credit from your spouse's and figure out what needs to be done to maintain or restore your reputation when it comes to your finances. To protect yourself from mounting debt, Credit Canada says the best things you can do include removing your spouse as a secondary cardholder on any credit cards and freezing joint credit card accounts while keeping up with the minimum payments until the court can address the repayment of debt.)

Pension Valuation and Splitting

Every asset and possession you have will be divided, including your pensions, though the specifics may vary from province to province. Ontario's law, for example, stipulates that each spouse is entitled to a share of the other spouse's pension that was earned during the marriage. Married couples who separate and divorce in Alberta are entitled to fifty percent of the value of the benefits earned during the period of joint accrual. In Nova Scotia, work pensions are considered to be matrimonial property under the Matrimonial Property Act. Your lawyer will be able to tell you whether you're entitled to a portion of your ex-spouse's work pension, how much you're entitled to, and the pension law that applies to your situation.

At this point, once you have the final agreement or court order, a request is made to the pension plan administrator to divide the assets. How it's divided and paid out depends on the situation and the type of plan. You often will have the choice of including the value of the pension in the equalization payment or dividing your pension separately. You really need the advice of a legal and financial professional before you agree to a pension division.

Canada Pension Plan (CPP) Contributions

The CPP contributions you and your ex-spouse made during the time you lived together can be equally divided after divorce. This is called "credit splitting." The federal government says eligibility for CPP credit splitting depends on when you divorced or separated and whether you were married or common-law. You have to apply to the government for a credit split — it doesn't happen automatically (there are forms to fill out, of course). You're eligible for it if your marriage ended in annulment or divorce, you lived with your ex-spouse for at least one year, and you've given Service Canada the necessary information. CPP credits can be divided even if one of the spouses didn't make any CPP contributions. If you live or work in Quebec, the Quebec Pension Plan (QPP) provides similar benefits. If you've contributed only to the QPP, you can find information on how to apply and eligibility rules on Retraite Québec's website (www.retraitequebec.gouv.qc.ca).

Dividing Your Finances

According to the Financial Consumer Agency of Canada, the first step in separating your finances is figuring out what you own and owe, both as individuals and as a couple.

Dig for and collect important paperwork: you'll need to record the names of your financial institutions and account numbers for chequing and savings accounts, loans, insurance, investments, and credit cards. It's key to have copies of:

- recent pay stubs
- statements for loans
- three years' worth of income tax returns
- investment statements
- receipts and bills for family related expenses
- life insurance policies

Prepare a list of what you own and what you owe, both individually and as a couple. Your assets can include:

- RRSPs
- RESPs
- separate or joint bank accounts
- insurance policies
- Tax-Free Savings Accounts
- your home
- CPP or QPP credits
- investments
- employer-sponsored pensions
- digital assets, such as cryptocurrencies
- businesses

You should ensure you know what everything is currently worth, and think about what it will be worth in the future. You can speak to your accountant or financial adviser to help you figure this out.

Your debts can include:

- a personal loan
- a line of credit
- mortgage

- credit card debt
- a car loan
- student loans

Any borrower listed on your loan agreement is responsible for the full amount that you owe. Let's say you have a credit card or line of credit jointly with your spouse and you are dealing with a federally regulated financial institution (FRFI), you have the right to receive disclosure information, including:

- information that explains the interest and other costs you will have to pay
- the same statements that the other borrowers receive on an ongoing basis

So, if you are a joint borrower on a credit card, you should receive a monthly statement about the account. From this, you will have a handle on the current status of the loan and what's owing, whether your spouse (the other borrower) is making payments and whether the terms and conditions have changed.

Deal with Joint Accounts and Joint Debts. Right Away

Any finances you share with your spouse should be dealt with immediately, including bank accounts, credit cards, lines of credit, and other loans. If you don't, say, close your joint bank account, you will both have access to whatever's in the account, and you'll both be legally responsible for repaying any debts. (Take note: This is true even if your separation agreement stipulates that one person is responsible for debts or can access funds in the account.) If for some reason you decide to keep a joint account open — for instance, if your mortgage comes out of a joint account — you should consider getting advice from a lawyer and perhaps make an agreement about what bills will be paid from the account and how much each spouse needs to deposit each month to carry these bills. If you don't already get information from your financial institution about your joint account, now is the time to ask to receive statements and other info.

Joint Credit Cards

Joint credit cards generally have a primary and authorized cardholder and only the primary cardholder has the authority to add or remove authorized users. If your ex-spouse is an authorized user on your credit card, remove him or her from the account. If you don't, they'll continue to have access to the account and you'll be responsible for money owing on the account. If you're a co-borrower on a credit card (you both have access to it and are equally responsible for money owing on the account), cancel it. Be sure to check your credit report after closing joint accounts. Canada's two credit report, credit scoring, and credit rating organizations are Equifax and TransUnion. Scores are between 300 and 900 and a higher score means you're a good risk. Lower scores mean you have taken on too much credit or have missed payments.

Update Your Beneficiaries

You'll need to review and update who you've named as your beneficiaries for the following:

- RRSPs
- TFSAs
- CPP or QPP
- employer-sponsored pensions
- Registered Retirement Income Funds (RRIF)
- Pooled Registered Pension Plans (PRPP)
- Life insurance
- Disability insurance

If you keep your ex-partner on as a beneficiary, he or she can still get benefits even though you're not together. If you are recently separated and you're unable to agree with your spouse about how your financial affairs will be managed prior to a final agreement, you should seek advice from a lawyer before making substantial changes to your financial affairs to ensure that you're not unnecessarily increasing your risk of litigation.

How to Update the CRA on Marital Status

Tell the Canada Revenue Agency (CRA) about your new marital status by the end of the following month after your status changed. For example, if your status changed in April, you must notify the CRA by May 31.

Tell the CRA if:
- you get married
- you become common-law
- you separated for more than ninety days (due to a breakdown in the relationship)
- you divorced
- your spouse or common-law partner died

The CRA will recalculate any benefits you receive based on your new status and adjusted family net income. The adjustment will start the month after your marital status changed.

You can update your status a variety of ways:

- online via CRA's My Account
- via this phone number in the provinces: 1-800-387-1193; or in Yukon, Northwest Territories, and Nunavut via this phone number: 1-866-426-1527
- via snail mail by filling out Form RC65 Marital Status Change and mailing to the office based on your location
  - If you're in British Columbia, Alberta, Saskatchewan, Manitoba, Northwest Territories, Yukon, or Nunavut: 66 Stapon Road, Winnipeg, MB, R3C 3M2
  - If you're in Ontario, New Brunswick, Newfoundland and Labrador, Nova Scotia, or Prince Edward Island: Sudbury Tax Centre

Post Office, Box 20000, Station A, Sudbury, Ontario, P3A 5C1
- If you're in Quebec: Québec Jonquière Tax Centre, 2251 René-Lévesque Boulevard, Jonquière, QC, G7S 5J2

Transferring Registered Plans

You might have to divide registered savings plans you own, including:

- RRSPs
- TFSAs
- RRIFs

You can find out how to divide these plans on the CRA's website. An accountant can also help you do this.

Issues to Discuss and Questions to Ask Your Accountant when Getting Separated or Divorced

Spousal and child support: These will be itemized in your separation agreement. Spousal support is a tax deduction to the person paying his or her spouse, and taxable income to the spouse who receives the support. You have the option to pay spousal support in lump-sum payments; speak to your accountant about which is best for you and your financial situation. Child support doesn't have tax ramifications. (Learn more about child and spousal support in Chapter 5.)

Canada Child Benefit (CCB): this is based on the adjusted family net income so both spouses' incomes are considered by the CRA to calculate the CCB.

Divorce and Taxes

The Canada Revenue Agency (CRA) considers you separated for tax purposes when you live apart from your spouse or common-law partner for more than ninety days. The CRA doesn't consider you separated if you've continued to live together in the same home. (For example, if you're sharing the family home for the kids but not living as a married couple, you are separated but the CRA doesn't see you as separated for tax purposes, including for your Canada Child Tax Benefit (CCB) or your Goods and Services Tax/Harmonized Sales Tax (GST/HST) benefits.

Trading Assets

Consider real estate, investment properties, retirement accounts, stocks and bonds, pensions, and antiques. When you divide your home (and other properties, if applicable), savings, pensions and investments, you're dividing your assets. Paying your former spouse their half of the assets is called an equalization payment. You are allowed to transfer an RRSP or RRIF without tax consequences if you meet the necessary conditions (if you're living separated and apart; you make transfers according to the terms of the separation agreement; the recipient is seventy-one years old or younger; and you file Form T2220 and the agreement with the CRA within thirty days of the transfer). All assets are not created equal, and accountants can advise on hidden tax costs that might be associated with an asset that will be transferred in the divorce.

Estate Planning and Separation

You'll want to think about estate planning if you choose to be separated from your spouse and not get a legal divorce. According to Ontario's Succession Law Reform Act, any reference to a former spouse in your will is revoked if you've opted to get a legal divorce. This provision protects your interests. Please check your appropriate provincial/terri-torial resources (link available in the glossary/resources section) for specifics if you live outside of Ontario. The thing is, there are no pro-tections in place for those who only decide to get separated, and it's actually a pretty common misconception to think that just because you're separated, your ex-spouse won't inherit anything if you pass away. If you don't have an update to your will and you pass away, your ex-spouse maintains his or her entitlement under the will. The experts say a simple way to understand this is if you own property together and you've separated, the property will go to the ex-spouse automati-cally. You can prevent this from happening by updating your will with your lawyer so your portion goes to your children, parents, siblings, or whomever you choose. It's a good idea to speak to an estates lawyer about your will after you separate.

As for Darla and Bryan, Darla says she learned everything she needed to know about divorce the hard way. "My advice to others who are going through separation and divorce is to remember that you are worthy and deserving of wanting the best for you and your children. Educate yourself as much as you can. If you do not know something, do not assume. Contact a professional who does know the answers, like lawyers and accountants. I devoured everything I could get my hands on in terms of rules, requirements, laws, procedures, etc. Document and keep records of everything. Do not let your emotions rule you. Focus on your future, your rights and entitlements. I am not saying you should be a bloodsucking vampire and take just to take, but do not bend. Stay strong. The person you are divorcing is not the person you were in love with. It is the strangest thing — they look the same, but it is not them. And even if this person is horrible, they are still the parent of your child. Do not disrespect them or talk badly of them when the child is present. Children have enough to deal with; do not involve them in your battles.

"You should also take care of yourself. I suffered from insomnia and lost thirty pounds. My anxiety was unbearable. I would pace all day like a lion at the zoo. Always on edge. I would just do circles around the house. I could not calm down. Take the time and figure out who you are in your new life. Do not jump into a relationship. Focus on you and your family. Get counselling. Best thing in the world. It helped me so much; I wish I had done it sooner. Forgive yourself. We are not perfect."

CHAPTER FOUR

Support

HILARY AND PHIL WERE TOGETHER twenty-three years and married for eighteen. They've been separated for two years, but their divorce isn't final yet. Theirs hasn't been an easy marriage — they were like two peas in a pod for many years, but things changed following the death of one of their three daughters twelve years into their marriage. Hilary says there was more than one reason for the eventual dissolution of their union: "I had an affair many years ago and that trust was never earned back, maybe that's what led us on this path, but who can know. But that's when it started — financial infidelity. He constantly lies about money. Constantly."

She says, "We never had the same beliefs about money. He liked to spend and felt he worked hard enough to enjoy what he earned. He always spent way more than we had and used many credit cards — some I didn't even know about. I learned of huge credit card bills that he lied about and eventually learned he didn't pay the Canada Revenue Agency for his own business taxes and HST, so we owed more than $60,000, which I learned about just months before I asked for a separation. He constantly lied about what things cost — he'd tell me a car repair was $500, but then I'd find the bill for $900. He bought lavish gifts and trips all on credit and we were drowning paycheque to paycheque. I wanted to save, but he spent all of our money and was horrible when it came to sticking to a budget.

When it came time to figure out how she'd go about filing for divorce, Hilary said she settled on a lawyer just to keep Phil honest. "I had never trusted him with money and I worried he was lying about what he had or that he had hidden money away. I also learned, through disclosure, that he had more debt on credit cards that he wanted to include in our equalization. I never knew. I also fought to have his business debt reduced to fifty percent in equalization because I felt it was his issue, not mine, and the amount included his interest and penalties for not paying and lying. Eventually I won these issues."

Things didn't get any easier — there were arguments about spousal and child support. "He pays, but my spousal support should've been more than child support ... He fought to make sure I didn't get more than he was paying for the kids. He told me I'm not worth it. See, he was the major breadwinner during our marriage, and I worked small part-time jobs while raising our kids, including the one with serious medical issues who passed away. He was able to climb the corporate ladder while I did the work at home and with the kids. He was also laid off several times during our marriage, sucking our savings and any bonuses he got. He lost his job twice during our separation too, so he didn't pay support for one year of our two-year separation. When we first separated, he lost his job five days later. We had nothing in savings and I was working full-time again. We lived together. He ended up taking money from our accounts and from our kids' Registered Education Savings Plan — I was livid. Then he took his girlfriend, who I didn't know about at the time, to Cuba over the holidays with our money and my kids' RESPs. He travelled three more times on our dime while not working or paying me. It was horrible."

Child Support

Child support is based on the Federal Child Support Guidelines, which are regulations under the Divorce Act. There are also provincial and territorial child support guidelines, though they are generally the same as the federal guidelines. (Quebec has its own child support model.)

Federal Guidelines

Although they are called guidelines, the Child Support Guidelines are law and they are used to determine child support when parents separate and divorce. Their main goals are:

- to reduce conflict and tension between parents by making the child support calculation objective
- to come up with a fair standard of support for children so they benefit from both parents' incomes
- to encourage settlements by offering guidance and to make the legal process more efficient

Federal guidelines say it's best for everyone involved, especially the children, when parents can agree on how they'll deal with child support without having to go to court. It's often more stressful, time-consuming, and costly to go the court route where a judge will make the decisions. The government's guide can help you work out an agreement together, and it can give you an idea of how much support a judge would order under federal guidelines if you opted to take your ex-spouse to court. If you can't agree or want your agreement put into a court order, you can apply to go to court.

Who Can Help?

There are many different types of professionals who can help, including mediators, lawyers, valuators, and accountants who specialize in working with parents on separation agreements and child support issues and arrangements. You can also visit your province's or territory's family justice services online. Lawyers, of course, can give you legal advice about your situation. They will tell you about your legal rights and responsibilities, your parenting responsibilities, how the court system works, how family-dispute resolution works (arbitrators, mediators, etc.), and your options for how you'll resolve differences with your ex-spouse and co-parent. Many provinces and territories have referral services that offer consultations with lawyers or other legal advisers for free or at a reduced rate. (You can also contact your local legal aid office to see if you qualify.) It can also help to speak to friends or family members who've been through divorce. And finally, you should consider hiring an accountant — these professionals can help because how your order or agreement is written will likely have an impact on your taxes and the benefits you can claim.

Dos and Don'ts for Parents Under the Divorce Act

1. You must act in the best interest of your children. It's a parent's duty to act in the best interest of his or her child, regardless of whether you have a parenting order from a court that specifies your parenting time or if you have an old custody order or agreement (made prior to March 1, 2021, when the Divorce Act was updated).

2. You must protect your children from conflict to the best of your ability. Whether your case goes to court or you are able to negotiate in mediation, parents shouldn't share details of the financial or parenting issues with their children.

3. You must try the family-dispute resolution process. According to the Divorce Act, it's imperative to try to resolve your case through a family-dispute resolution process, such as mediation. This is the less expensive route to take and it's more collaborative for all parties than going to court. The Divorce Act acknowledges that this route isn't the safest or best option in all cases. If there's been domestic violence or abuse or you have other safety concerns, speak to your lawyer about your options.

4. You must keep your legal adviser and the court up-to-date with accurate and complete information. You'll have to give the court all the information they need, ensuring your records are kept up-to-date. For example, if you get a raise at work, your income information must be updated with the court so fair and accurate child support can be calculated.

5. You have a duty to comply with all court orders. If you don't, there are serious legal consequences. If your situation or your children's

situation has changed and you no longer believe the court order fits your situation, you should go back to court to have the order revised.

Eight Steps to Calculate Child Support From the Federal Child Support Guidelines ... With Examples

Step 1: Determine which guidelines apply to you.

If you're divorced or have applied for a divorce, the federal guidelines apply to your situation unless you both live in a "designated" province. There are three designated provinces: Quebec, New Brunswick, and Manitoba. These three provinces have arranged with the government of Canada to use their own guidelines in divorce cases when both parents live there. Here's how they break down:

- If both parents live in any Canadian province or territory other than the three mentioned above, federal guidelines apply to you
- If both parents live in Quebec, New Brunswick, or Manitoba, provincial guidelines apply to you
- If both parents live in different provinces or territories, even if one or both are in designated provinces, federal guidelines apply to you
- If one parent lives in Canada and one lives in a different country, consult a legal adviser. Federal guidelines apply, but in some cases guidelines of the other country might apply as well
- If you and the other parent have never been married and you both live in Canada, provincial or territorial guidelines apply to you
- If you are married and have separated but you're not divorcing and you've already resolved child support under provincial or territorial guidelines, those provincial or territorial guidelines apply to you

Example: Paul and Alison

Paul and Alison are getting a divorce. They live in New Brunswick with their two kids, Nicholas and Luca. New Brunswick is a designated

province and the whole family lives there, so the province's child sup-
port guidelines apply to Paul and Alison.

Example: Jay and Sarah
Jay and Sarah are married. They have one child named Sebastian. They've
been living apart for the last couple of years. Jay lives in Manitoba and
Sarah lives in Ontario. They are getting a divorce. Since they live in
different provinces, the federal guidelines will be used to determine the
support amount for Sebastian.

Step 2: Determine the number of children who require support.
The situation or age of a child can affect how you calculate child support. According to the Divorce Act, you must support any child of the
marriage — any children you had together while you were married,
including adopted children who:

- are under the age of majority* and are still dependent; or
- have reached the age of majority* but can't become independent
  due to disability, illness, or another cause

* the age of majority is eighteen in Alberta, Saskatchewan, Manitoba, Ontario, Quebec, and Prince Edward Island
* the age of majority is nineteen in British Columbia, Yukon, Northwest Territories, Nunavut, Nova Scotia, New Brunswick, and
  Newfoundland and Labrador

However, you should seek proper legal advice to better understand how
your own facts and circumstances relate to child support.

Example: Sam and Pritha
Sam and Pritha have three kids: Amanda is twenty, Avery is sixteen
and Paige is fourteen. The couple is getting a divorce. They know the
federal guidelines apply to their situation (they both live in British
Columbia). Paige and Avery are both under the age of majority and are
still dependent, so Sam and Pritha both have an obligation to support

them. Amanda is over the age of majority and is independent, so she is not entitled to support.

If you are acting in place of a parent to the child of your partner or spouse (such as being a step-parent) you or a court could decide you should pay support for that child.

Example: Tom
Tom is close to his stepson, Jake. He's been in his life since he was a toddler — he was married to Jake's mother back then. Their marriage ended in divorce, but Tom still sees Jake and is helping to raise him. Jake's mother and Tom decide Tom will act in place of a parent to Jake and he'll pay support for him. They ask their lawyers to help them come up with an appropriate amount.

For kids who are over the age of majority, the same rules can be used. Or, you might both agree to base support for an older child on his or her needs, means and other circumstances, as well as the ability for both of you to contribute financially.

Example: Matthew and Lou
Matthew and Lou are getting a divorce. They have a twenty-one-year-old daughter, Zoey, in her third year of university. They go to mediation to help them come up with an agreement about their daughter's support. It is determined that Zoey is still dependent on them while she continues her education. They look at Zoey's needs, means and other circumstances, and their ability to help her financially. They decide that some of Zoey's financial needs will be covered by her Registered Education Savings Plan and student loans, plus Zoey has a job, so she will use her part-time earnings. They also decide they are both able to continue contributing financially to help support their daughter.

Step 3: Determine the parenting time arrangement.
The federal guidelines use three terms to describe parenting time arrangements: 1) shared parenting time; 2) split parenting time; 3) majority of

parenting time. For the purposes of child support, these refer to the time the kids spend with each parent — they don't refer to who makes the major decisions.

Shared parenting time:
You share parenting time if your kids spend at least forty percent of their time with each of you in a year. Note that there is no standard for calculating forty percent. Courts have approached this in different ways and you should seek advice from a lawyer if you're seeking to make any changes to your child support based on the amount of time your children are in your care.

Example: Melissa and Ben
Melissa and Ben are divorcing. They want to come up with the best situation for their kids, Zach and Willow. They decide the kids will spend alternate weeks with each parent — one week with Melissa and one week with Ben. In the summer, the kids might spend two weeks with Melissa, then two weeks with Ben. Zach and Willow are spending at least forty percent of the time with each parent, so they have a shared parenting time arrangement for child support purposes.

Split parenting time:
You will have a split parenting time arrangement if you have more than one child and you each have the majority of parenting time with at least one of the kids.

Example: Sigi and Ilan
Sigi and Ilan are getting a divorce. They are having a difficult time deciding on their parenting arrangements, but will do what's best for their three children: teenager Jacob, and preteens Ethan and Lily. Because Jacob is very close with his father, the couple decides (with a mediator's help) that Jacob will spend the majority of the time with Ilan. The two younger children will spend the majority of the time with Sigi. So, Jacob will spend more than sixty percent of the time with Ilan and Ethan and Lily will spend more than sixty percent of the time

*with Sigi over the course of a year. They will have a split parenting time
arrangement.*

Majority of parenting time:
You have the majority of parenting time if your kids spend more than
sixty percent of the time with you over the course of a year.

Example: Natasha and Yu
*Natasha and Yu are getting divorced. They have three kids: Kaitlyn,
Sadie, and Simon. The ex-couple agrees that Natasha will continue
to live in the family home and the kids will stay with her so they're
close to their school and friends. The kids will see Yu on weekends and
holidays. When Natasha and Yu calculate how much time the kids will
be with each of them over the course of a year, they determine they'll
be with Natasha about seventy percent of the time and with Yu about
thirty percent. This means Natasha has the majority of parenting time
for child support purposes.*

If it's determined your situation requires another arrangement (other
than the three listed above), consult your legal adviser for assistance in
figuring out what's best for your children.

Step 4: Find the correct table.
The federal guidelines have child support tables for every province and
territory. After you determine which guideline applies to you (you did
this in Step 1), you can determine which table in the guidelines applies
to your situation.

The various tables show basic child support amounts that depend
on the income, number of kids, and which province or territory the
family lives in. There's a federal table for each province and territory
because child support amounts are based partly on provincial and territorial tax laws.

- If both parents live in the same province or territory, use the
  table for that province or territory

- If you live in different provinces or territories and one parent has the majority of parenting time and the other parent must pay support, use the table for the province or territory where the paying parent (the payer) lives
- If you live in different provinces or territories and you share or split parenting time, use the tables for both provinces or territories where you live to determine what you would each pay to the other parent

Step 5: Calculate your annual income for child support purposes.
Note: Calculating your income can sometimes be difficult, especially if you're self-employed or your income fluctuates. Now is a good time to get financial help from an accountant.

Whose income is needed:
Sometimes both parents' incomes will be necessary and sometimes it's only the payer's income that's required. You'll need to calculate both incomes if you share or split parenting time, if one of you is acting in the place of a parent to children, if there are extraordinary expenses, if either of you claims undue hardship, or if your child is at or over the age of majority and you calculate child support in a different way than you would if the child was under the age of majority.

You also might need to calculate both incomes if the paying parent earns more than $150,000 per year (see more below on this).

What's needed to calculate income:
- your income tax returns for the last three tax years
- the notices of assessment and reassessment from the Canada Revenue Agency for each of the last three tax years
- you might also need to share your most recent pay stub or a letter from your employer stating how much you make; your corporation's financial statements if you're self-employed or control a corporation; income you received from employment insurance, workers' compensation, disability payments, social or

public assistance; or information about your corporation's pre-tax income if you're a shareholder, officer, or controller of a corporation

If you don't provide this information, a judge can order you to provide the information, impose a penalty or set an income that is appropriate in your circumstance.

Calculating income:
Under the federal guidelines, you can: 1) agree in writing about your annual income or 2) apply the specific rules set out in the federal guidelines. Under these rules, the total income shown on line 15000 (line 150 for 2018 and prior years) of your most recent income tax return or your notice of assessment is where you should start. You might need to adjust your income if it varies a lot from year to year, you received a one-time payment (like a bonus), you live in another country where tax rates are different or you pay or receive spousal support. You are obligated to continue to provide income information if the other parent requests it (they can do this once a year). It's key to remember that you need to keep each other informed of changes to your income to ensure you're paying the right amount of support based on the most accurate, up-to-date information. If, for example, you get a raise and you don't inform the other parent of this change to your income, a court order could make you make retroactive child support payments.

Example: Holly and Jared
Holly and Jared divorced three years ago and they agreed to share parenting time of their kids, Bella and Albert. At that time, they agreed Jared would pay child support to Holly, since he was the higher earner. They also agreed (in writing) that they would each share their income information every year. Jared's industry was hurt during the pandemic and his company downsized. He kept his job, but at a reduced salary. He tells Holly what happened, and they both agree to change their child support agreement based on Jared's new income information.

Step 6: Find the table amount

Now that you know the number of kids being supported, the table you need to use, and the income the child support amount will be based on, you have to find the table amount that matches your income and the number of kids being supported. The basic child support amount depends on your parenting time arrangements. For information on the guidelines for your province or territory, please see the following link: www.laws.justice.gc.ca/eng/regulations/SOR-97-175/index.html.

Shared parenting time:

The rules for calculating child support are different in this case. You'll need to find the amount in the tables that each of you would pay for your kids if the other parent had the majority of parenting time. This may be referred to as the set-off amount of child support. You'll also need to take the increased cost of shared parenting time and the means, needs and other circumstances of each parent and child into account. Here's an example:

Example: Winnie and Pat

Winnie and Pat are getting divorced. They live in Yellowknife. They have agreed to share parenting time for their two kids, Keira and Koen. Winnie makes $20,000 a year and Pat earns $30,000 a year.

To figure out a support amount, they look at the table to find out the amount they'd pay for two children if the other parent had the majority of parenting time. Based on their incomes, Winnie would pay $306 per month and Pat would pay $469 a month for two children. Next, they subtract the lower amount from the higher amount to find the difference: $163. When they look at the expenses each will be paying when the kids are with them, they decide Winnie will have more expenses than Pat. They agree that it's fair for Pat to pay an extra $30 per month to help because he earns more. They agree that the amount of support Pat will pay to support the two kids is $163 + $30 = $193 per month. Note: if you are paying the set-off amount of support, you should seek the advice of a lawyer or accountant to ensure that your *separation agreement or order accurately reflects the arrangement for CRA purposes.*

Split parenting time:
First, you'll need to check the table for the province or territory where you live and find the table that correlates to the number of kids you have. You'll find out how much support you would pay for the kids that are with the other parent for the majority of parenting time. Once you've found the amount that each of you would pay, subtract the lower amount from the higher amount and that's what the higher earner pays.

Example: Aisha and Isabelle

Aisha and Isabelle are getting divorced. They have three kids, and they live in Ontario. When they divorce, they decide the older child will live with Aisha and the two younger kids will live with Isabelle. Aisha will have the majority of parenting time with one child and Isabelle will have the majority of parenting time with two children for child support purposes. They use the table for Ontario to find out how much support Aisha would have to pay for the two children living with Isabelle. It shows that based on her income of $50,000 per year, she would have to pay $755 per month. They also use the same table to find out how much support Isabelle would have to pay for one child living with Aisha. It shows that based on her income of $40,000 per year, she would have to pay $359 per month. Then they subtract the lower amount from the higher amount and get a difference of $396. Aisha will pay $396 per month.

Majority of parenting time:
On the correct provincial or territorial table, find the amount of support that matches the paying parent's income and the number of kids being supported.

Example: Adele and Marc

Adele and Marc are divorcing. They live in Ontario, but Marc moves to Quebec and Adele stays in Ontario with their three kids. They agree that this arrangement is in the best interest of the kids, and Marc will pay child support using the federal tables. Since they live in different provinces, they use the federal table for Quebec, since that's where Marc lives and he's the payer, to determine the basic amount of child support.

Marc earns $75,000 per year. The table shows that the basic amount of child support for three kids based on his income is $1,404 per month.

Income over $150,000:
The child support tables only show an amount for the first $150,000 of income. You have two choices for determining how much child support should be paid on the portion of income that exceeds the $150,000: 1) you can multiply the amount of income over $150,000 by the percentage shown in the table for the province or territory where the paying parent lives; or 2) you can agree on an additional amount of support based on means, needs and other circumstances of your children, and your financial ability to contribute. Add the table amount for the first $150,000 of annual income to the amount you decide for the portion over $150,000 to get the basic child support amount. If you earn more than $150,000 per year, you should consult a lawyer to ensure that you are paying an appropriate amount of child support.

Example: Daniela and Jack
Daniela and Jack are getting a divorce. They live in Alberta. They have one son, Shawn. They agree that Shawn will live with Jack and Daniela will pay child support. Daniela earns $175,000 per year. In Alberta, the basic amount of child support that someone who earns $150,000 would have to pay for one child is $1,318 per month. The two agree to use the percentage shown in the table to determine how much additional support Daniela should pay on the portion of income over $150,000. The percentage for one child in Alberta is 0.84 percent.

$175,000 - $150,000 = $25,000 (portion of income over $150,000)

$25,000 x 0.0084 = $210 (support payable on income over $150,000)

$1,318 + $210 = $1,528 (combined total)
Daniela will pay $1,528 per month for child support.

Step 7: Determine if there are special or extraordinary expenses.
Step 6 was a starting point. Now you have to figure out whether there are any special or extraordinary expenses in your situation. If you find there are, you'll need to figure out the amount you should be paid in relation to these specific expenses. Typically, these expenses are paid proportionately to income. The federal guidelines define special or extra-ordinary expenses (also known as section 7 expenses) as:

- necessary, because they're in the child's best interests; and
- reasonable, given the means of the parents and the child in light of the family's spending patterns prior to separation

They can include:
- childcare expenses that you have because of a job, disability, illness, or educational requirements for employment if your child spends the majority of the time with you
- the portion of your medical and dental insurance premiums that provides coverage for your child
- your child's healthcare needs that exceed $100 per year if the cost is not covered by insurance (counselling, medication, eye care, or orthodontics, for example)
- expenses for post-secondary education
- extraordinary expenses for your child's education or any other educational programs that meet your child's needs
- extraordinary expenses for your child's extracurricular activities
- any other expenses that you agree are not covered by the monthly Table amount of child support.

It's always best if you agree on which special or extraordinary expenses are reasonable and necessary in your situation. The federal guidelines say you can even include expenses like university tuition that you expect in the future. It's all about keeping your child's best interests top of mind. If you can't agree, you might want to consider third-party help from a mediator or lawyer.

Details to consider:
When figuring out your child support agreement, include the particulars of each expense, such as:

- what it's for (dance, hockey, etc.)
- the total cost
- how much you'll each contribute to the cost
- the date payments are due
- whether the payments will be made directly to a service provider or as a reimbursement to the other parent
- any other relevant information

Calculating your share:
Generally, parents share the amount determined for the expenses in proportion to their incomes. You can also agree to share the amount in a different way.

Step 8: Determine if there is undue hardship.
The amount of child support determined under the federal guidelines, when combined with other circumstances, can create undue hardship for your child or yourself. If this is the case, a different child support amount may be appropriate. Either parent can claim undue hardship.

To prove this, you must show two things: 1) that your circumstances would make it hard to pay the required amount or support the child on the amount of support you receive; and 2) that your household's standard of living is lower than the other parent's household's standard of living.

According to the federal guidelines, these circumstances can cause undue hardship:

- unusually high costs associating with exercising parenting time with a child (like needing to travel long distances)
- unusually high debts you reasonably incurred to support the family before the separation or to earn a living

- a legal duty to support a dependent child from another relationship
- a legal duty to support any other person, such as a former or new spouse, who is too ill or disabled to support himself or herself.

Comparing standards of living:

There's a worksheet attached to the federal guidelines you can use to compare the standards of living of the two households. It's based on the standard-of-living test in the federal guidelines. You can also use other ways to compare the standards of living of your households.

If you were to go to court, the judge would most likely apply the test found in the federal guidelines, as well as the income of each household and other members of the household, including your new spouse or common-law partner, any kids living with you, any person who shares or helps reduce your living expenses and anyone whom you are legally required to support or be supported by.

If the standard of living is lower in the household of the parent claiming undue hardship, the claim might be accepted and the child support amount could change. The amount could be higher or lower than the amount already calculated.

Common-Law Relationships and Child Support

Kids of parents living in common-law relationships have the same rights as children of married couples. You can ask for support if you and your former partner have or adopt a child together, or if your spouse treated your child from a former relationship as their child while you lived together. The amount of support you receive can be determined via negotiation, collaborative family law, mediation, or arbitration. If the issue can't get resolved, you can ask a judge to order your spouse to pay for support. (The amount is set under the Child Support Guidelines.)

Two Big Misconceptions about Child Support

1) "My husband doesn't make very much money, but the kids live with me the majority of the time. Will he get away with not paying child support because of his income?" No. Not making much money

doesn't necessarily mean that you're not going to have to pay child support. It definitely impacts how much child support you'll pay, which means it could be $50 or $100 a month. The point is, you'll pay something if the other parent is the primary caregiver, no matter how much you make. Note: There is no child support payable for payers who make less than $12,000 per year.

2) "Since I have the kids most of the time, I get all the parental authority." Not so. Some people think that even if the child lives with them most of the time — they have the right to decide to enroll their kid in private school, etc., but in the absence of an agreement or order stating that one parent has sole decision-making authority, both parents share decision-making, whether they have equal parenting time or not. They are to share decision-making responsibilities when it comes to education, health, religion, and major extracurricular activities. It doesn't matter who the child lives with or who will pay for the expense. The other parent must agree to an expense before it will be shared. If the parents don't see eye to eye and there's a good case for, say, the child going to private school, they can ask for a court order.

Common Questions About Child Support (From Ontario's Ministry of the Attorney General)

Q: I'm pretty sure my ex-spouse is earning more now than when the child support order was made. How can I find out?

A: The person paying support must provide the recipient with confirmation of his or her income every year on the anniversary of the support order, unless they've specifically agreed not to exchange income disclosure each year. If there's a difference in earning, you can agree together on a new amount of support (you can do this on your own, with a mediator, or with your lawyers). If you can't agree, you'll need to go to court to have a new amount set by bringing a Motion to Change.

Q: My ex-wife is playing games about when I can see my kids and she's not following our schedule — for example, she sent the kids on playdates when it was my turn to see them. Why should I pay child

support if I don't get to see them when I'm supposed to?

A: The law is clear here. You have to pay support no matter what happens with your parenting time arrangements. That said, you still have a right to have your parenting time arrangements honoured and respected. Bring this up with your lawyer, mediator, or a family counsellor and work with them and your ex-spouse to ensure you're getting your time.

CHILD SUPPORT IN QUEBEC WITH SHERI SPUNT AT SPUNT & CARIN IN WESTMOUNT, QUE.

"In Quebec, we have our own form called the Schedule 1. On that form, you input Parent 1's income, Parent 2's income, then you indicate how many children you have and how many days the child/ren will spend with each parent. The form generates how much child support is to be paid on a bi-weekly or monthly basis. For example, if you're in a shared parenting arrangement, the parent who earns less is going to receive child support from the other parent. If one parent has all the parenting time, the form will generate how much child support will be paid based on how much time the child/ren spend with each parent. If the parents make the same income and it's a fifty-fifty schedule, there's going to be no support paid from one parent to the other."

Additional Information

Changing an order or agreement:
You can change a written agreement together if you both agree to the changes. If you can't agree, a mediator or collaborative lawyer might be able to help you.

Enforcing support:
The provinces and territories are responsible for enforcing child support. If you need help enforcing an order or a written support agreement, contact your provincial or territorial maintenance enforcement program

(these go by different names such as the Family Responsibility Office). There's also a section about this on the Department of Justice Canada website.

If you have more questions:
There are a variety of resources at the end of this book, as well as on the Department of Justice Canada family law websites. You can find information about provincial and territorial family justice services, enforcement services, and services that refer to legal advisers and Public Legal Education and Information organizations.

You can also call the Department of Canada Family Law Information line at (613) 946-2222 or (1-888) 373-2222.

CHILD SUPPORT FROM A LAWYER'S PERSPECTIVE
WITH JESSICA CHAPMAN, DARTMOUTH, NS

"Child support is black and white. There are federal child support guidelines that all provinces follow closely and it's very difficult to get around them. From my side, it definitely prevents a lot of litigation on this issue.

"Federal guidelines take how much you make — let's use line 15000 on your last income tax return — and asks how many kids you have and what province you live in. If you use the government's child support table, you'll get an exact amount to the dollar that you'll have to pay. If I had a client who was a payer and didn't have the children in his or her care most of the time, I would tell him or her they'd have to pay that amount. Period. Like I said, child support from my perspective is pretty black and white.

"What's interesting about child support, which I think a lot of people take issue with, is that it does not matter what the recipient's income is. So, if you have a doctor making $500,000 per year, she will have to pay the same amount of child support to the primary care parent whether he's a waiter making $20,000 a year or also a doctor making $500,000. That's legislation that says you need to provide support to that person in accordance with your earning capacity.

"Extraordinary expenses or Section 7 expenses fall under section 7 of the federal guidelines: these include uninsured medical expenses, dental, expensive extracurricular activities, braces, glasses, post-secondary education, or private school. From my perspective, these often cause a big headache. The law can be unclear as to what should be considered a Section 7 expense, so lots of people will say, for example, a parent should be able to pay for hockey registration that costs $200 out of child support because it's not an extraordinary amount of money. The other parent might say, 'I shouldn't be required to pay in addition to the child support — I'm already paying for regular extracurricular activities.' But what if it's not $200 and it's $2,000 because the child is in a premier hockey league? At what point does that cost become something the payer should have to be responsible for? The law in that way is unclear and can be the source of a lot of back and forth. From my perspective, it ends up wasting a lot of people's legal fees fighting about it. Extraordinary expenses can be a big headache. And making a claim for them can be a headache."

Spousal Support

Spousal support (sometimes referred to as "alimony" or "maintenance") is money that one spouse might have to pay to the other for financial support after they've separated or divorced. It's usually paid monthly, but can be paid out as a lump sum. One spouse might have to pay spousal support for one of these reasons set out in the Divorce Act:

- to compensate a spouse who sacrifices his or her ability to earn income during the marriage;
- to compensate a spouse for the ongoing care of children, over and above any child support obligations; or

- to help a spouse in financial need arising from the breakdown of the marriage

Spouses who receive support have an obligation to become self-sufficient or self-supporting.

Either spouse can ask for spousal support, but in most cases, it's requested by the spouse who has the lower income. A judge will consider many factors to determine if it should be paid, including:

- the financial means, needs, and circumstances of both spouses
- the length of time the spouses have lived together
- the roles of each spouse during the marriage
- the effect of these roles and the breakdown of the marriage on both spouses' financial positions
- the ongoing responsibilities for care of the children (if applicable)
- the goal of encouraging a spouse who receives support to be self-sufficient in a reasonable period of time
- any previous orders, agreements, or arrangements that were made about spousal support

Under the Divorce Act, spousal support is most likely to be paid when there's a significant difference between the spouses' incomes after they separate or divorce. But this isn't always the case — a judge can decide that the spouse with the lower income isn't entitled to support. This could be the decision if the spouse has a lot of assets, for example.

Under provincial and territorial law, a common-law partner might be eligible for spousal support. (This is true for all of Canada except for in Quebec, where common-law partners or "de facto spouses" are not entitled to spousal support when they separate.) Entitlement in these cases could depend on how long they've lived together before separating. (In some provinces and territories, common-law couples must live together for two or three years before either is eligible for support.) Your provincial or territorial Ministry of Justice or Attorney General will have this information, and so will your lawyer or legal adviser.

Chapman says spousal support is not nearly as straightforward as child support. "Child support is legislated, but there's a lot more variation in the court with spousal support. The big issues with spousal support are, first of all, entitlement. So, before you start wondering how much money you're going to get, you have to find out whether you're entitled to spousal support. From my perspective, if the court has said there is financial dependence for a period of time, the court will not allow the higher-earning spouse to wake up one day and say, 'I'm done financially supporting you.' It's not in the interest of public policy for somebody to be financially dependent on someone one day and all of a sudden be cut out completely the next. Our federal Divorce Act specifically says that the recipient has an obligation to make efforts to become self- sufficient. There is a judge who famously said, 'spousal support is not a pension for life.' It is supposed to be something that helps the other party become self-sufficient."

How It's Calculated

The experts agree that this is actually one of the most difficult areas of family law. There are a plethora of factors that need to be looked at to figure out a fair and appropriate amount. Most Canadian courts and family lawyers use the Spousal Support Advisory Guidelines when calculating this support. (That said, it's not law. The Federal Child Support Guidelines are law, but these guidelines are not.)

Common Questions about Spousal Support

Q: Is periodic, or monthly, spousal support taxable?

A: Periodic, or monthly, spousal support is generally taxable as income for the recipient, and it is generally tax-deductible for the payer. Child support is neither. It comes out of the payer's net income.

Q: Are both child support and spousal support paid at the same time?

A: Many people pay this way, yes. But the Divorce Act prioritizes the payment of child support, which means if you don't have enough money for both spousal support and child support, spousal support may be temporarily reduced to zero until your income increases or there is a change in the amount of child support payable.

Q: **How long will spousal support need to be paid?**

A: There's no straight answer here because the duration depends entirely on the facts of the case, such as how long the spouses were married and lived together, as well as their ages at the time of separation. Spousal support might be paid for a short time, or it could be what is referred to as indefinite support, which does not necessarily mean that it will never end, but that it will continue until there's a change in circumstances and the court makes a different order.

Q: **When can I stop paying it?**

A: You can't randomly or unilaterally decide when you want to stop paying support. You have to continue to pay unless the order is changed by a court; you and your ex-spouse agree to change the agreement; or the conditions for stopping payment (as set out in an order or agreement) have been met.

   A judge can change a spousal support order when justified by a major change in the circumstances of either spouse. If the payer, for example, loses his or her job and can no longer afford to pay the amount that was ordered, a court can decide the support order should be changed. If you have a spousal support agreement with your ex-spouse, you both have to consent to any changes to your agreement before they can take effect. If there's a specific end date on your order or agreement, you're within your right to stop paying on that date. So, for example, if your order or agreement states you must pay support that will end on December 1, 2021, your spousal support obligation ends at that time.

   "The main factors taken into consideration when determining spousal support are the length of the relationship, the incomes of the parties, and the age of the parties when they separated. If you have a ten-year relationship and the incomes of the parties are $60,000 and $30,000, then the $60,000-earning spouse will probably have to pay support to the other, depending on the circumstances. However, the age at which they separate becomes very important. If they separate when they're sixty-five, the prospect of that sixty-five-year-old finding self-sufficiency is slim if they haven't had a career, if they haven't been working, and they are at retirement age," says Chapman. "I say that because if you're together from age twenty-five to thirty-five and you're thirty-five years old, you have your entire working life ahead of you and you have lots of time to become self-sufficient. And if I was representing the payer, I would say, 'OK, we agree to pay this amount of spousal support, but we want to know your plan — what is your plan to become self-sufficient? Are you going back to school? Are you in some kind of internship program?' Because the scariest thing about spousal support when you separate, from the payer's perspective, is that it can be claustrophobic and very scary to not know when this will end. The rule of thumb for the duration for how long spousal support usually takes place is anywhere from half the length of the relationship to the full length of the relationship. So, if you are together for ten years, that means you're looking at five to ten years of spousal support. If I am representing the payer, I'm telling them we should do everything we can, including maybe paying that person more if it means an absolute termination date that's not subject to variation. On the flip side, if I'm representing the recipient and he or she doesn't have a concrete plan of how they're going to support themselves, I will tell them, 'Let's attempt to keep the timeline on your support open-ended because we don't know where you're going to be in a year or two or three years or four years.' It's a very nuanced area of the law."

Q: How do I know how much support I should ask for?

A: First, figure out the details of your income and expenses. List what you spend on food, household expenses, and other things like medication, dental, clothes, transportation, car expenses, insurance, gifts, entertainment, pet food, etc. These expenses can be included when you're determining how much support you need. Your lawyer can help you with this and can explain the support advisory guidelines that apply to your situation. The Ontario Ministry of the Attorney General suggests visiting www.mysupportcalculator.ca.

Q: I've lived with my partner for ten years. Most of that time was spent at home taking care of our kids. We never married. Can I get support for myself?

A: Yes, you can ask because common-law spouses have a right to ask for support if they've lived together for more than two or three years (depending on the province or territory) or if they've lived together less than two or three years but have had kids or adopted together.

Misconceptions About Spousal Support

Rosanne Walters, an accountant and certified family mediator of Walters Financial Forensics in Delta, BC, says there are common misconceptions about how spousal support works. "There are guidelines regarding ranges of spousal support based on many factors, including the length of the marriage, income disparities and the role of the partners during the relationship. Another is that spousal support is usually negotiated between the partners," she says. A common myth is laid out below.

Myth: I'm off the hook when my ex remarries or moves in with someone else.

Not so. Remarriage or cohabitation with someone new can be one of the factors in deciding whether spousal support will continue to be paid, but it's not a guarantee that it will end support — it really depends on what the other spouse is entitled to. So, if the recipient spouse was a stay-at-home parent for years during his or her marriage with the paying spouse, it won't matter if he or she decides to get hitched again because of the years spent contributing to the family (raising children and maintaining the household) in non-monetary ways.

BACK TO HILARY AND PHIL. There were plenty of concerns when the two separated, but one of the major issues was Hilary's worry that she wouldn't be able to do everything that needed to be done on her own. "I did it, and so can anyone else," she says proudly. "The day we separated I went to the bank for a full printout of our joint accounts.

I got my own bank account, credit card, and a $10,000 line of credit in my name. I started an RESP for the kids and a Registered Retirement Savings Plan for myself with only a little bit of money. My credit was good. His wasn't. I ended up having to leave our family home — it was toxic. I used my line of credit for first and last and for three months' rent while we sold our marital home. I borrowed from my parents to pay for my lawyer, but that was it. When our house sold, we each took $100,000 while the balance was being decided on. I paid off every last debt from my lawyer, credit card (used for furniture for my new house), my parents, and my line of credit. I was debt-free. I saved the rest, added to my RESP, RRSP, and got a Tax-Free Savings Account. I got a huge tax return and invested that, too. Not surprisingly, my ex ran out of money fast and begged to have more released. Two years later, we finalized all equalization, and he has nothing left to show from our marital home. I have an amount to invest until I'm ready to buy or save for my future. I'm proud of this.

"I spent about $25,000 on a lawyer. The time it took to finalize the divorce was longer than I'd ever imagined it would be, but she was good. Everything I was angry about in the beginning didn't matter to the legal system. We did five court conferences but no trial. We settled it back and forth at the end, exactly two years from the separation date. Now I've filed for divorce. We are fifty-fifty now; he makes three times what I make. The law exists for women like me who gave up careers to raise kids and let their spouse travel and climb the ladder. I have zero guilt taking his money. It helps me provide a nice house and standard of living for my girls that's similar to our old life and similar to the way their dad has his home."

CHAPTER FIVE

Balancing the Books and Recovering Financially

RABIYA, FORTY-TWO, AND FARHAN, forty-seven, were married for eleven years and have been separated for about a year and a half — that's when Farhan moved out of their shared home. "I just felt like we'd drifted apart," he says. "We were different people when we met and started dating, but once we had kids and life became different, I was the only one who matured and moved into a new stage in our lives. We never fought very much — it just seemed like we were living two different lives. Passing ships in the night and all that. I parented, organized the house and wanted to spend time as a family while she wanted to continue living our pre-kids life: out drinking all weekend," he says.

The biggest problem in their marriage, says Farhan, was money. "I am extremely frugal and my ex has no concept of saving at all. It was a constant battle. She always wanted to spend and when we did buy things, she wanted the best money could buy while I wanted the cheapest and most economical. We usually came to a middle ground, but the process wasn't fun. I'm a budgeter and she preferred to spend as she made it." Take, for example, the time the couple needed a new fridge. "I just wanted a basic model — something that would do the job. But no, she wanted the top-of-the-line model that we absolutely could not afford. We went back and forth on the pros and cons — the biggest con being our inability to spend so much money on an appliance — and we found a middle ground, but it was a fight." He also says he's a frugal shopper for kids' clothing, for example. "I was in charge of buying the kids clothes and I'd usually buy from big-box stores when there were sales on, but she always gave me a hard time about it. She wanted the kids dressed in brand-name clothes. I can't tell you how often I tried to explain why it wasn't worth it — kids outgrow their clothes, our boys are hard on their shoes, etc. — but she never dropped it."

Farhan says he was worried about what the separation would do to his two kids, and he was concerned about finances if he was on a single salary. Still, he left Rabiya.

You already know that everything about divorce is hard — including financial issues. You might be the spouse who is paying ongoing child and spousal support to your ex-partner. You might also be the spouse who lost half of your assets. There's no denying this is a stressful time — it's tough emotionally and socially, but it's also difficult financially.

You're probably wondering "what now?" What comes after all of this, now that you're no longer officially tied together financially? "For good and ill, it can be a long process of disentangling yourself financially and personally, on every level. On the one hand, that's difficult because you continue to be meshed with this person in a challenging situation. It takes time to develop your independence from one another, depending on the length of the relationship and the nature of the marriage. In the traditional example of marriage, your lives are enmeshed — one minute you're totally connected in all ways and the next minute you're not. You need time to get through it. When it comes to the finances, people have to be extremely methodical about the way they separate. If you're the spouse who hasn't been managing the finances, there will be a learning curve. Be reasonable with yourself and educate yourself in this area. In the end that will feel great because you'll be more independent and empowered," says accountant Kelly LaVallie.

Tanya Sterling is a Victoria-based chartered professional account-ant, a chartered financial divorce specialist, a trained mediator and coach, and a financial neutral who specializes in divorce. She says her clients generally display one of three perspectives when it comes to working through the financials for separation. "The first is from a place of fear and uncertainty — these are the clients who lack trust in everybody and everything, things are spiralling, they are super overwhelmed with the whole process and the coaching is a larger element for these clients. The second are those who think they have all the answers. They come to table with an analysis already laid out, and wonder why the other person hasn't come on board with their way of thinking. Our work here often revolves more around getting everyone on the same page. The last includes couples who are feeling okay with the situation, they might be unsure and just need some clarity around what the options are and some guidance to walk through — they absorb it as they go and integrate financial changes right away. Part of the process, regardless of each client's narrative, includes getting a better understanding of where they are now, where they want to go and how they'll get there. For everyone, in any situation, once we work through the first step, you can see people begin to feel more and more empowered as we continue to work through the process. Once the direction becomes clearer and they know what they are dealing with, even when still sitting with uncertainty or disagreement, you can see once they are clearer about what the options are and have a better understanding of how those options impact them, you can really hear their voice start to come out in an empowered, respectful way. People are no longer fighting against each other, but instead fighting together to find an outcome that they can both live with and move forward. Some people just want the answers and they want to get out of there, but the magic comes from working together to find the answers. The law in many areas is so grey that opinions can vary greatly from one lawyer (and judge) to the next, so it becomes even more important to walk through all angles and figure out a solution that puts what is important to both people in the spotlight while considering the information from a legal context. This, in addition to taking a more farsighted view where they will benefit so much more from a process with someone who understands their financial situation very closely, and benefit from some coaching to discover what their roadblocks, patterns, and skillsets are so they can move forward in a financially independent way," Sterling says. "We work together to come up with a plan, as well as help to implement the plan, monitor the plan, and recheck the plan if and when needed. If something's not working or there are emotional triggers coming up surrounding the rollout, that's where the coaching can come in. This is why it's key to work with an appropriately trained expert and supporting team who you can trust have the skillsets to navigate the path forward."

There are ways you can get your finances in order after separation or divorce.

Where to Start

1) Create and/or review your budget: This is necessary so you can better handle your expenses. When you go through a separation or divorce, you will no longer be sharing your household expenses; you might be on the hook for making support payments; you'll likely have extra expenses when it comes to setting up your new home; and you will need to pay your legal costs. To help you create a household budget, there are many free options offered by organizations such as financial institutions (discussed in Chapter 2) and others such as the Ontario Securities Commission (www.get smarter aboutmoney.ca/calculators/cash-flow-calculator) to help you easily create a household budget. CPA Canada also gives you access to complete your own budget worksheet, by visiting www.cpa canada. ca/finlitresources, under money management worksheets.

2) Get a copy of your credit report and review it carefully. You can do this by contacting any of the three major credit bureaus, including TransUnion, Equifax, and Experian. Alternatively, many financial institutions also offer their clients free access to credit reports depending on your banking package. By checking your credit

report, you will be able to gext a full picture of your credit and identify all your individual and joint debts. Furthermore, the credit report will show you which accounts have you listed as an authorized user. While only the primary account holders are usually held liable for these liabilities, it is wise to remove your name from these types of account to avoid any issues later.

3) Get your own bank account: if you don't already have your own chequing or savings account, now's the time to open one. In addition to opening a bank account, you'll want to make sure you've closed any joint accounts you've identified in your credit report. This would include any joint bank accounts, credit cards, and loans that you've obtained over the years together. To do this, contact lenders and ask to have your joint accounts either transferred into individual accounts, or if there's no balance, just close them. This reduces the risk of having new charges that both you and your ex-spouse will be responsible for.

4) Update your banking information: If you're getting new credit cards and bank accounts, inform your employer (for your direct-deposit paycheques), as well as any company you deal with that makes automatic withdrawals or debits (your internet provider, alarm company, streaming-service account, etc.). Don't forget to let the Canada Revenue Agency (CRA) know, if you get direct deposits when it comes to your Canada Child Benefit, GST/HST benefits, and income taxes refunds. In fact, the CRA requires individuals to tell them about a change in marital status by the end of the following month after your status changed. For example, if your status changed in March, you must tell them by the end of April. The best way to change your marital status with the CRA is by registering and logging in through My Account through the CRA web portal, by phone or by mail. To find out more information please visit the following link, www.canada.ca/en/revenue-agency/services/child-family-benefits/update-your-marital-status-canada-revenue-agency.html.

5) Update your personal information: If you're moving from the matrimonial home, update your address for all financial accounts, including

the CRA. And if you've made the decision to change your last name post-divorce, you'll have to update that information too.

6) Build your personal credit history: if your bank accounts, credit lines, and credit cards were in your ex-spouse's name, you likely don't have much of a credit history, which is generally very important if you need a loan in the future. For instance, you'll need a good credit history if you want to be approved for a credit card, mortgage, a place to rent, and a job (employers can ask for your credit history). You can start building your individual credit history by opening a new credit card under your name. This might not seem like a priority after dealing with the financial worries caused by your divorce. However, establishing your personal credit sooner rather than later is important for your financial future. After being approved for credit, there are a number of things you can do to help build your credit history, such as paying down your debt at a faster pace, and increasing your credit limit. Building your credit score can be a long process, especially after a divorce, so patience is key.

7) Buying and selling property: while you were married, you may have owned your family home. After a divorce, you may have the longing to purchase another home. But the truth is, it's expensive to buy and sell property, so you don't want to make a rash decision when it comes to real estate. There are a lot of things to consider before you decide what housing options best meet your new lifestyle and needs:

Is it the right time? Like many other things in life, the housing market has its peaks and valleys and has its high and low seasons. Depending on when you finalize a divorce, the timing can significantly impact your decision to buy another property. For example, if you finalize a divorce at the beginning of a recession, it might be wise to defer either selling your matrimonial home if housing prices have dropped significantly or buying another property if your job situation is insecure. If you're able to stay with family temporarily, you'll have more time to figure out where you want to go and how much you can afford. Another option is to rent a home temporarily to give you some time to think about your housing options. This way you can sit back and research your desired neighbourhoods, or even wait until there is a slowdown in the housing market, to give you the opportunity to purchase something you like at a more affordable price. Renting temporarily may also give you some time to save money to put into a down payment on a home.

Rent vs. buying for the long run: everyone has different circumstances that impact different aspects of their lives, including being able to afford to purchase a home. Many people might feel social pressures to buy a home vs. renting, especially after a divorce. However, when it comes down to it, one of the main things to consider is affordability and managing your household cashflows. If you're in a situation where most of your money will be going to service your mortgage and you won't have anything left over to build a cushion for those emergency expenses, this is probably a good indicator that renting a more affordable home might be the smarter option as you adjust to your new post-marriage life. As well, you might want to take the time and get comfortable with your new life before you make any big decisions like buying a new home. Your household income has likely gone down, and it might be wise to take the time and get used to your new financial dynamics by renting. As a renter, you won't have the same expenses as a homeowner, and you're not usually responsible for the repairs and maintenance of your home.

8) Look at your benefits coverage: if your health coverage was under your ex-partner's group plan, there's a good chance you'll no longer be covered. Consider whether you should make changes to your own group plan and whether you want to take out private healthcare coverage. After a divorce, one of the most important things to consider is whether your former spouse has adequate life, disability, and critical illness insurance, especially if you are relying on them for ongoing spousal and child support payments. When people get divorced, there is often still an element of financial dependence through ongoing child or spousal support obligations. That's why it's common when negotiating the terms of a divorce and separation to request that the spouse with the ongoing obligation of child and spousal support payments to secure that obligation

in the event of death or disability. The most common way to do this is by purchasing life, disability, and critical insurance policies on the life and health of the former spouse. It's not complicated to determine the amount of the insurance benefit required, as it's based on the amount and duration of the future child and spousal support payments. For example, if the separation agreement requires your former spouse to pay you $50,000 a year in spousal and child support payments over a duration of 10 years, you may want to make sure that you are listed as the beneficiary on a $500,000 life insurance policy ($50,000 x 10 years) on the life of your former spouse (insured person). Therefore, if your former spouse passes away, you will receive a $500,000 payout. If your former spouse didn't have a life insurance policy or any assets and then passed away, you would be left with nothing and would no longer be able to depend on receiving any more child and spousal support payments, which would most hurt you financially.

Insurance can be a complicated topic, that's why you should speak to a qualified finance professional about your insurance needs.

9) Update your will: if you no longer want your spouse to be your executor or trustee, decide who you want to name as your power of attorney, and decide who should make healthcare and financial decisions if you're unable to. As for beneficiaries, who will you make the beneficiaries of your estate, life insurance, Registered Retirement Savings Plans, and Tax-Free Savings Account? Your lawyer or qualified financial adviser can help you decide what makes the most sense for your situation.

10) Set new goals: you might be wondering how you'll make it on your own, but don't give up — it's time to set new financial goals. Consider where you want to be financially. Do you have debt you want to pay off? Do you want to save for your children's education? When do you want to reach financial independence and retire? It will be easier to decide what to do if you ask your qualified financial professional for help — you don't have to do this on your own.

How to Create a Budget

(from the Financial Consumer Agency of Canada) Note: the Government of Canada has a budget calculator online (www.itools-ioutils.fcac-acfc. gc.ca/BP-PB/budget-planner), which we used to explain the steps below. There are also calculators available on the websites of most financial institutions. You can also create your own budget spreadsheet.

Step 1: List the income you expect to earn over the course of a year and average it on a monthly basis. Below is a helpful worksheet to help you keep track of these items:

Income	
Salary after taxes (take-home pay, self-employment/business income)	$
Employment insurance	$
Pension benefits (e.g. CPP, OAS, etc.)	$
Employer pension benefits	$
Investment income	$
Income from child support	$
Government child benefits	$
Disability and other insurance benefits	$
Other income (If you have another source of income, for example, rental property income, you can add it in.)	$
Total Income	$

Step 2: List your assets which are available to be converted into cash. These numbers can include:

Assets Which Are Available to Be Converted into Cash	
Chequing or savings account	$
Emergency cash funds	$

Assets Which Are Available to Be Converted into Cash cont'd	
Registered accounts (e.g., RRSP, TFSA) and non-registered savings accounts	$
Home and other property	$
Vehicle(s)	$
Other assets	$
Total	$

Step 3: List your expenses incurred over the course of the year and average it on a monthly basis. These numbers can include:

Expenses	
Debt repayment (credit card, line of credit, personal loan, student loan)	$
Housing (mortgage payment or rent, home equity line of credit, property taxes, condo fees, repairs and maintenance, capital/appliance upgrades)	$
Communications (internet, phone, cable, streaming services, and memberships)	$
Food (groceries, restaurant/takeout, food appliances)	$
Insurance (life, medical and dental, disability or accident)	$
Transportation (car loan/lease payments, gas, maintenance, parking, public transportation, ride-sharing services)	$
Childcare (daycare, babysitting)	$
Education (tuition, text books, school trips)	$
Recreation (travel, club memberships, kids' toys, event tickets, sports gear)	$
Personal care (hair, cosmetics, spa)	$
Clothing (including kids' clothes and accessories)	$
Medical (dentist, other specialists/treatments)	$
Pets (food, veterinarian)	$
Fees (bank, credit cards, professional memberships and dues)	$
Gifts and donations	$

Expenses cont'd	
Taxes and other government fees	$
Total Expenses	$

Step 4: Review your results. Here you'll get guidelines that tell you what Canadians generally spend or save for each category. If you're using the calculator on the Financial Consumer Agency of Canada's site, you'll see thumbs up (which means the amount you're spending is within the average range), a warning sign (when the amount is slightly above the average range), or a stop sign (this amount is above the average range). You can use these signs to help you focus on where you can cut costs. (Of course, these are just general guidelines and everyone's situation and goals are different, but at least you'll get a jumping-off point.). Alternatively, you can use the worksheet below to help you calculate your net cash flows:

Monthly Cash Flow	
Total Income	$
Total Expenses	$
Net Cash Flow (Total Income — Total Expenses)	$

Step 5: Review next steps. In this section, you'll get personalized suggestions based on your situation and goals and what you've entered into the budget calculator. You'll quickly see whether you have money left over each month or if you're overspending.

How to Stick to Your Budget

A budget is a spending plan that takes into account both your current and future income and expenses. Having a budget helps keep your spending in line and ensure you are saving enough to meet your future goals. To stick to your budget, the Financial Consumer Agency of Canada says to:

- keep a record of your bills and receipts
- limit your spending so you stay within your budget

- update the budget with any necessary changes, such as a pay raise, new bill, etc.
- compare your budget to what you're actually spending in each category at the end of every month. You'll quickly see where you need to cut back
- evaluate the budget often (if your spending varies from the budget, readjust your figures). Set a reminder in your calendar to review regularly—it will help you stay on track

Ask yourself these questions:
- Are there big differences between your spending and your budget? Why?
- Which categories have the biggest differences? Why?
- Are the differences likely to happen every month or are differences due to an unusual or one-off situation that seem to be recurring?
- Can you save enough to pay off debt and reach your financial goals?

"Most of the professionals I work with focus on getting through during the actual separation and divorce, and then, once the agreement is signed, their involvement is over. When working in a collaborative process, it can sometimes be the beginning of a new chapter, where the professionals continue to be there to support the family if issues arise again in the future. In a collaborative process, ideally, as part of the separation, there may have been a budget analysis review and a projection prepared to forecast the impact of the settlement options, which helped to clarify what sort of decisions needed to be made to help find an ideal outcome, including what kind of lifestyle they each can move forward with the added support to help them realize those goals should they need it.

"It's important to ensure everyone is on the same page from the beginning and that they understand and agree with the process. Different people paddling in different directions is never a good thing. This helps to streamline the information gathering and risk analysis and sets the right tone for option analysis. After we have confirmed onboarding and the information has been gathered, I meet with both parties individually to go through financial situations, and that's when we talk about goals, potential legal topics to be discussed when attending the next meeting with counsel as well as other financial pieces that may need to be considered.

"I then sit down with the lawyers and the clients, and we go through all the information together and part of my role involves guiding the lawyers to provide legal advice around each of the topics and to moderate discussions that tie the information to the client's needs and goals in order to assist in developing a solution that works for their family. In my experience, having the right team at the table makes all the difference when looking to serve the best needs of the family.

"When needed, we spend the time to look at budgets, projections, coaching clients around how they see their future, and identifying what's holding them back from moving through emotional or financial roadblocks. In our discussions, it is important to be an active listener and help support them to move through the uncertainty. For instance, if someone says, 'I've never been good with money,' or 'I'm bad at this stuff,' it is important to focus on that sort of language to see what the underlying narrative is and to see if they can reframe their perspective in order to become a more active participant in their own lives.

"By the time we're looking ahead at their financial futures, the team has typically been able to develop a good relationship. We are then able to better understand the financial interests, goals, and roadblocks as well as come up with options around how to work through them, because we've had those discussions. It's important to take the time to ensure each of the clients understands where they are: We look at a current snapshot including credit rating, a summary of their assets and liabilities, their budget, a projection, and I say, 'Here's where we are' and in talking about that projection, I am curious about things like, 'What do you envision happening in the next year? Two years? Five years? Ten years?' With those discussions, that's where the coaching comes in, so they're really conscious and aware when making those decisions and taking those steps to create a future reality instead of believing that their future is just going to 'happen to you' by chance, it's a future they are actively developing because we're able to visualize that future and put plans into place so they can take small steps (or big, if they want) to make those outcomes happen."

As for Farhan and Rabiya, their marriage was definitely over, and things actually got worse. "We went through mediation initially; however, Rabiya chose not to show up and they stopped seeing us. Then I saw a lawyer independently and she still hasn't. It wasn't and isn't fun. The mediator I was using was very helpful, but the lawyer I found was terrible. It was extremely expensive, and she was constantly pushing to try to make more money." The couple ended up splitting their house fifty-fifty, but there's been a huge problem since they moved apart: Rabiya isn't paying child support. "She has gotten herself in trouble and is couch-surfing at friends' houses. She doesn't have a place of her own, she's not working, and she doesn't have money. I survive on the money from the sale of our house and my job, and I doubt she will ever help me. She's spent her half of the house already."

Post-Divorce Checklist

Once the financial and parenting agreements are in place, there are a number of administrative items to complete.

- Ensure that you keep several copies of your separation agreement or divorce order in a safe yet accessible place.
- Revise your will and change your beneficiary designations on all pertinent paperwork such as Registered Retirement Savings Plans, insurance policies, investments, etc.
- Consider naming a new power of attorney.
- Consider whether or not to register with the maintenance enforcement program in your jurisdiction (these go by different names such as the Family Responsibility Office in Ontario) to ensure payment of support.
- Joint credit cards and accounts should be closed and distributed accordingly. If maintaining the account, remove one name. Note: when coming off debts, it's important to receive written evidence

of release of those debts in the form of a release letter. Having your name off the account may not be sufficient, and it's in your best interest to have written documentation.

- Establish credit with new credit cards, points, and rewards cards.
- Ensure automatic payments or withdrawals from bank accounts are updated before closing accounts.
- Distribute and divide property and debts. This includes the marital home and any contents, other property and personal items, bank accounts and investments, consumer debt and credit cards, and pension and registered retirement funds (complete T2220 transfer form to divide assets if applicable).
- Change title, registration, and transfer insurance on any vehicles and licence plates that need to be updated.
- If moving, redirect mail and update all accounts with the new address.
- Fill out any name-change applications, if applicable.
- File form RC65 to notify the Canada Child Benefit program and GST of the change in your marital status. This can also be updated when you file a tax return or if you have access to CRA's My Account. Your next tax return should be filed with the appropriate marital status.
- Update your benefits (or apply to an individual group benefits plan for yourself).
- Split the Canada Pension Plan credits online at servicecanada. gc.ca.

CHAPTER SIX

Going Forward

MARRIED FOR TWELVE YEARS, BONNY and Julie got married in their forties. They were together about fourteen years total and didn't have any children. Bonny says Julie is a good person, but there was obvious "wear and tear" over the years. "Julie kept switching jobs. She'd never stay in one for too long — maybe two years at the most. It was challenging to bring it up to her. I ended up not bothering because it would frustrate both of us. I ended up resentful. A few years ago I reconnected with someone I'd known in university and she had qualities Julie didn't have. So I decided to leave — I took a chance and now I can say it was wise. Jamie and I are happy," she says.

Money didn't play a huge role in Bonny and Julie's divorce. They had three accounts, including a joint account in which they'd each put in $500 from every paycheque, and they had their own accounts. Bonny says their personal accounts were used for things like hair, nails, books, personal hobbies, and nights out with their own friends. "We just closed our joint account. We didn't ask each other for our own savings or pension. I didn't ask Julie for her father's money — she had the money from the sale of the condo when he passed — and Julie didn't ask me for a split in my pension or savings. It was amicable." It truly was — there were no lawyers involved and no mediators. The divorce cost $600. "I can't really say I had any financial concerns when we separated. My mother was there to help if I needed it, and I was working full-time so there was money coming in. I think I was just happy to be on my own. We had no issues around spousal support because neither of us asked for any. She still works and was always able to pay rent, even though her jobs changed constantly. She was good with money — I'm a bit of a spendthrift."

Bonny has a new partner and things are going well. Julie is also in a new relationship — in fact, she got remarried several months ago. "I'm happy for her," Bonny says. "I don't know if remarriage is in my future. At this point I'm happy with my partner and I'm enjoying being independent. I don't know if I want to be tied to someone else like that again. I'm undecided."

It's okay to be undecided like Bonny. It's also okay to decide to remarry like Julie — you just have to take a few things into consideration. The Ontario Securities Commission says remarrying or living with someone new means you'll need to adjust to a new financial relationship too. There are a bunch of questions newlyweds find themselves asking after they say "I do," including when to save versus when to spend, how to combine daily finances, how much debt is too much, and which investments they should make. (These are questions that should be asked prior to getting hitched, but I digress. CPA Canada's book *Love and Money: Conversations to Have Before You Get Married* by Wallace M. Howick, FCPA, FCA, is a wonderful resource to gift friends and family before they say their vows.) Second marriages, though, bring on even more money issues. For example, if your new partner is also divorced, are either of you paying child support? Spousal support? Is one of you buying your matrimonial home from your ex? What about your pensions? If you have kids, you'll find there are even more expenses, such as post-secondary school tuition.

We don't have new stats on how many divorced Canadians decide to remarry, but according to Statistics Canada back in the late-2000s, about thirty percent of divorced people were living in common-law unions, and thirty-one percent of those people said they intended to remarry. None of those people expected their first marriage to end in divorce, and it's safe to bet all of them hope their next trip to the altar will last. Since financial issues play such a huge role in marriage, you'll want to ensure you spend time planning and communicating about money to avoid some of the problems, anger, misunderstandings, and resentment you might've had in your first marriage.

What You Need to Remarry

There are legal requirements you'll need to deal with before remarrying. This information specifically explains the process in Ontario, but many provinces and territories are similar.

First, you'll need an Order for Divorce that's granted by the Superior Court of Justice or Unified Family Court. This order, of course, is the formal document granted by the court that ends your marriage legally. You should receive a copy of the order either via your lawyer or in the mail. Second, you need a Certificate of Divorce, which is issued the day the divorce is finalized. (Most of the time, this is thirty-one days after the Order for Divorce is granted.) You can get this document via your lawyer or directly from the court. When you apply for a new marriage licence, the clerk will need to see your Certificate of Divorce as proof you're no longer married.

There are other things to consider as you plan your financial life after divorce. Here are five areas you'll want to take note of:

1) Plan for your future: You'll want to think about what life will look like moving forward. This includes looking at mutual goals when it comes to finances. Many financial coaches and accountants have worksheets you can fill out together to gauge where you are when it comes to looking ahead at your financial life together. (OK, it's not super sexy, but it's on the must-do list.) All that said, you should brace for challenges. The experts say it's best not to get fixated on issues from your past marriage — just because your ex-spouse lied about money, it doesn't mean your new partner will do the same. They also say it's integral to respect each other's point of view and to discuss individual goals, as well as relationship goals.

2) Manage cash flow: Tanya Sterling, an accountant and expert on divorce and finances, says she often sees conflict which stems from

choices and values around money. "Where I often see the disconnects include if one person is a spendthrift and the other is a saver, or when one person knows everything about their money situation and the other person knows very little, and sometimes the person who knows everything doesn't want to share the details with the other person. When that kind of situation is in play, sure, it's about money, but it's also about so much more — it's about mistrust," she says. It's true — she says it's the day-to-day issues with money that can cause the most financial stress in a relationship. When it comes to second (or third, etc.) marriages, cash flow is a tough subject if one or both of the couple are paying child and/or spousal support tied to a previous marriage. Living expenses will also need to be looked at if there's a child or children from a previous relationship living with the new couple. Parenting and money could cause tension here. For example, if one parent believes in paying his or her kids to do chores and the other parent doesn't, or if one parent restricts extracurricular activities to one per season and the other parent allows his or her children to engage in multiple activities or sports. "You might benefit from working through some of these thorny topics with a financial coach to create a plan that helps you both achieve your individual and family goals — a plan that falls in line with your values. If these issues are not addressed, the outcome is often that each person is pushing their own agenda, which causes underlying tension that may affect the relationship overall. There are so many decisions that need to be made, including whether you'll manage your money separately and each contribute to a joint account for expenses, or if you'll completely combine your incomes. There's no right or wrong answer here — it depends on what you're most comfortable with and ideally, one you've had an honest discussion about in advance.

3) Talk about it: if you're both looking to enter into a second marriage, you might find there are financial differences, such as an imbalance of money (which can lead to an imbalance of power). And if money was a contentious topic in your last relationship or in your divorce, it might make it even more difficult to discuss. This is where a

financial neutral is great — you can get help to talk about money more openly and honestly. A third-party adviser might suggest signing a marriage contract (often called a pre-nuptial agreement or domestic contract) to help you both feel more comfortable. More on that later.

4) Think about retirement: ask yourself some key questions like when are you planning to retire? What does that look like with a new spouse? Are you both planning on retiring at the same time? What will it cost? Is your ex-spouse entitled to any of your pension benefits or retirement savings? What about your new partner's ex-spouse? The experts suggest running the numbers individually and together. The good thing about doing this now is you'll create more clarity around where you see yourselves in the future.

5) Look at estate planning: financial advisers suggest looking at what the financial impact would be on you individually and as a couple if one of you has a serious illness, disability, or if one of you passes away. Now's a good time to look at your will and how you'll divide your estate. This could get confusing and complicated if there are kids from previous marriages. In order to avoid sticky situations, your best bet is to consult a financial adviser and decide how the division will be written up in your will and your partner's will. You can also consider purchasing life insurance and naming your kids as the beneficiaries. Still, it's worth your peace of mind to talk to a financial expert and/or estate-planning professional.

Marriage Contracts and Cohabitation Agreements

A marriage contract is a legally binding agreement that can be entered into between two people prior to or after getting married that sets out an agreed upon set of rules if the couple separates or divorces. Common-law couples can also enter into a similar agreement, but it's called a cohabitation agreement. Lawyers can prepare these agreements for you, but you should each have your own legal advice before signing. Couples enter into these agreements so they can control who gets what if the relationship ends or if they end up getting separated or divorced.

What can be included in a domestic contract:
- division of property on separation or death
- ownership of property (what's owned separately and what's owned jointly)
- spousal support obligations
- beneficiaries for life insurance policies, RRSPs or pension plans
- pets and what will happen to them in the event of separation

What can't be included in a domestic contract:
- decision-making and parenting time
- child support

Bonny and her partner, Jamie, have never been happier. They've moved in together and have enjoyed seeing their lives become intertwined. Jamie's kids from her first marriage visit frequently, and the pair are enjoying raising their new goldendoodle. "I never could have expected this when I was going through my divorce — back then the sadness and anxiety took over and I admit now that I couldn't see past it. I didn't think my next chapter would be so bright, but it's taken healing. I gave myself time to reflect, heal and allowed myself to move on. My advice to those who are going through or have recently been through a separation or divorce is to know that there's light at the end of the tunnel. Yes, it's cliché, but it's true. I'm happy these days, and Jamie and I are thriving in our living arrangement. When I think back, I remember all that sadness — the worrying, the guilt, the upset — but it all worked out in the end. And that's what I think is the most important lesson — separation and divorce are hard on everyone involved, but they doesn't define you or your life going forward. Things can and will get better."

CHAPTER SEVEN

Glossary and Resources

Glossary of Terms

A

Access: Prior to the 2021 amendments to the Divorce Act, "parenting time" was referred to as "access". This term was used to refer to the amount of time the non-primary parent had with the children. When the Divorce Act talks about non-parents (e.g. grandparents) applying to spend time with children, it's called "contact."

Affidavit: A document that sets out facts that you must swear under oath or affirm to be true.

Age of majority: This is the age when a child legally becomes an adult in the province or territory where the child lives. It's eighteen in some provinces, and nineteen in others. If the child lives outside of Canada, the age of majority is presumed to be eighteen.

Annual income: This is the income earned from all sources used to calculate child support under the Federal Child Support Guidelines.

Arbitration: A binding process in which a dispute is settled by one or more arbitrators (private judges) who make a binding decision on the dispute. Arbitration is a form of Alternative Dispute Resolution.

Arrears: Child or spousal support that hasn't been paid; when the payer is falling behind on making support payments to the payee.

B

Best interest of the child: This is the test to decide what best protects children physically, emotionally, psychologically, and what's best for their well-being. It looks at their emotional health, the child's relationships with parents and family, and the impact of family violence. If you go to court, the judge considers the child's best interest in making all parenting arrangements.

C

Child support: All parents must support their children financially, whether or not they are the primary caregiver. Child support is the amount a parent pays after divorce to help the other parent support their children and includes a monthly amount and, often, a separate amount for special or extraordinary expenses. A child support agreement or order specifies the amount the parent will need to pay.

Child Support Guidelines: The laws, with rules and tables, used to determine how much child support should be paid when parents separate or divorce. The Federal Child Support Guidelines are regulations under the Divorce Act and apply when parents divorce. Provincial or territorial guidelines apply to unmarried parents.

Child support tables: These tables are included in federal, provincial, or territorial child support guidelines. The tables indicate the basic child support amounts based on income and number of children. There is a separate table for each province or territory to reflect different tax rates between the provinces and territories.

Cohabitation agreement: A contract made between unmarried partners — common-law couples — who want to live together but also want to protect their interests.

Collaborative family law: A process in which you and your lawyer, and your ex-spouse and their lawyer, agree to resolve their divorce outside of court.

Common-law relationship: An unmarried couple who lives together in a marriage-like relationship. The rights and obligations arising from this living arrangement vary between the provinces and federally.

Contested divorce: When both spouses disagree on some or all issues within their divorce. These issues are commonly disagreements about spousal and child support, parenting schedules, division of assets, etc.

Court order: A legally binding document signed by a judge that dictates the terms on which your separation will proceed such as child support, spousal support, and parenting arrangements.

Custody: In the 2021 updated version of the Divorce Act, the word "custody" was removed. It is now referred to as "decision-making responsibility."

D

Decision-making responsibility: This is the responsibility to make important decisions about your child's well-being, including decisions about education, healthcare, culture, religion, and significant extracurricular activities. If both parents have decision-making responsibilities, they have joint decision-making responsibility.

Dependant: This is someone who depends on you for financial support (a source of income), and could include a spouse, children, or an extended family member.

Divorce: The legal ending of a marriage. Divorces are granted under the federal Divorce Act.

Divorce Act: The federal law that governs divorce. It includes issues pertaining to divorce, including parenting time, child support, and spousal support.

Divorce certificate, divorce order, or certificate of divorce: You might need a certificate of divorce to remarry, to file for another divorce, or to confirm that your divorce has been finalized. To obtain this certificate, you must go to the court house where your divorce application was filed.

Domestic contract or agreement: A document that explains how spouses or unmarried people have agreed to deal with one or more issues arising from their relationship such as child or spousal support, property, or parenting. Domestic contracts can be made before moving in together, while living together or after separation. However, it is important to note that some issues cannot be pre-determined.

E

Excluded property: This is property that is not divided between spouses as part of the equalization of family property, and includes gifts and inheritances that one spouse received during the relationship (from someone other than his or her ex-spouse), as well as assets each spouse had before the relationship started. It can also include certain insurance payments. This is defined in each province's applicable legislation.

F

Family court: A division of provincial court that grants court orders under the provincial family law legislation for parenting arrangements, spousal support, child support, and other issues.

Family debt: This includes all debts spouses take on during the course of their marriage, including loans (from family and financial institutions), mortgages, lines of credit, credit cards, income tax, and other costs.

Family dispute resolution: This process is about settling your family law dispute out of court. Professionals in family law dispute includes lawyers, mediators, arbitrators, parenting coordinators, and counsellors.

Family justice services and programs: Private or public services and programs that help people dealing with issues stemming from separation and divorce.

Family property: This includes property you and your spouse own as of the separation date, and it includes your house, car, furniture, appliances, bank accounts, benefits, insurance policies, pensions, stocks, and other investments. Property is generally divided equally after separation, unless it qualifies as excluded property.

L

Legal adviser: A person who's qualified in a province or territory to give legal advice to someone or represent them in court. This is generally a lawyer, but in some provinces, it may include other professionals.

Litigation: The process of two opposing parties engaging in formal legal proceedings to settle one or more areas of dispute (usually through lawyers representing each party).

M

Maintenance enforcement: Legal actions taken to compel a person to comply with support requirements set out in a court order or written agreement.

Maintenance enforcement programs: Provincial and territorial programs that enforce child support obligations set out in a court order or written agreement.

Majority of parenting time: This refers to situations where a child spends more than sixty percent of the time with one parent.

Marriage: Marriage is a legally sanctioned union regulated by laws, customs, beliefs, and attitudes.

Marriage contract: Married or engaged couples can enter into marriage contracts (domestic contracts) that spell out rules for division of property and spousal support if the relationship breaks down.

Matrimonial home: Any property that was ordinarily occupied by the person and their spouse as their family residence at the time of separation may be a matrimonial home. It does not matter whether or not one spouse purchased it before marriage, or whose name is on the mortgage. This means that the value of the matrimonial home is divided between spouses when they separate or divorce.

Mediation: A voluntary, non-binding alternative dispute resolution process by which you and your ex-spouse work with a mediator — a neutral third party who is trained to help you reach an agreement out of court.

P

Parenting arrangements: The arrangements parents or guardians make about how they'll parent together. This includes the allocation of parenting time and decision-making responsibility.

Parenting time: The time a child spends with a parent or guardian. It involves being responsible for the care and supervision of the child. It is based on what the parents or the court determine to be in the child's best interest. Parents can decide how to divide parenting time and set it out in the separation agreement or it can be ordered by the court.

Pension: A regular payment to a retired person from an investment fund to which the person or their former employer has contributed.

Prenuptial agreement: see marriage contract.

R

Retainer Agreement: A retainer is a contract between you and the lawyer that forms a solicitor-client relationship. Note: the money you pay to a lawyer to secure their services is called a retainer fee.

S

Separation: Separation is when two people who have been living together in a marriage or in a common-law relationship decide not to live with each other anymore.

Shared parenting time: Situations where a child spends at least forty percent of the time with each parent over the course of a year.

Split parenting time: Situations involving more than one child where each parent has the majority of parenting time — more than sixty percent — with at least one of the children.

Spousal support: Support paid to a former spouse under an agreement or court order. It is sometimes referred to as alimony in some provinces.

Support payer: A parent or a spouse who has a legal duty to pay child or spousal support.

Support recipient: A parent, or a spouse who acts in the place of a parent, who is legally entitled to receive child support.

U

Uncontested divorce: This is where the parties are both seeking a divorce and they've already reached an agreement on all issues, such as parenting time, child support, spousal support, division of property, and decision-making responsibility.

Government Resources

Federal Department of Justice: Divorce and Separation: Where to Start: https://www.justice.gc.ca/eng/fl-df/divorce/wts-poc.html

Federal Department of Justice: Child Support: http://www.justice.gc.ca/eng/fl-df/child-enfant/index.html

Federal Department of Justice: Family Justice Services: https://www.justice.gc.ca/eng/fl-df/fjs-sjf/index.html

Federal Department of Justice: Parenting Arrangements: https://www.justice.gc.ca/eng/fl-df/parent/index.html

Federal Department of Justice: Spousal Support: https://www.justice.gc.ca/eng/fl-df/spousal-epoux/index.html

Federal Department of Justice: Fact sheets in various languages: https://www.justice.gc.ca/eng/fl-df/pub.html

Making Plans: A Guide to Parenting Arrangements After Separation or Divorce: https://www.justice.gc.ca/eng/fl-df/parent/mp-fdp/toc-tdm.html

Parenting Plan Checklist: https://www.justice.gc.ca/eng/fl-df/parent/ppc-lvppp/index.html

The Federal Child Support Guidelines: https://www.justice.gc.ca/eng/rp-pr/fl-lf/child-enfant/guide/index.html

Alberta Family Law: https://www.alberta.ca/family-law-assistance.aspx

British Columbia Family Justice: https://www2.gov.bc.ca/gov/content/life-events/divorce/family-justice

Manitoba Family Law: https://www.gov.mb.ca/justice/crown/family/law/

New Brunswick Family Law: PLEIS-NB • Public Legal Education and Information Service of New Brunswick: Family Law (http://www.legal-info-legale.nb.ca)

Supreme Court of Newfoundland and Labrador Family Division: https://court.nl.ca/supreme/family/index.html

Nova Scotia Family Law: https://www.nsfamilylaw.ca/

Northwest Territories Children and Families: http://www.justice.gov.nt.ca/en/browse/children-and-families/

Nunavut Justice: https://www.gov.nu.ca/programs/justice

Ontario Family Justice: http://www.attorneygeneral.jus.gov.on.ca/english/family/

Prince Edward Island Family Law: http://www.princeedwardisland.ca/en/topic/family-law

Quebec Couples and Family: https://www.justice.gouv.qc.ca/en/couples-and-families/

Saskatchewan Family Justice: https://www.saskatchewan.ca/residents/births-deaths-marriages-and-divorces/separation-or-divorce

Yukon Family Law: https://yukon.ca/en/family-law-information-centre

Government of Canada Divorce or Separation: https://www.tpsgc-pwgsc.gc.ca/remuneration-compensation/services-paye-pay-services/paye-information-pay/vie-life/divorce-seperation-eng.html

CRA Forms

T2220 Transfer from an RRSP, RRIF, PRPP, or SPP on breakdown of
    marriage: https://www.canada.ca/en/revenue-agency/services/forms-
    publications/forms/t2220.html

Other

Making a budget: https://www.canada.ca/en/financial-consumer-agency/
    services/make-budget.html

Budget Planner: https://itools-ioutils.fcac-acfc.gc.ca/BP-PB/budget-planner

Ontario Ministry of the Attorney General Resource List: https://www.
    attorneygeneral.jus.gov.on.ca/english/family/

Acknowledgements

Uncoupling wasn't an easy book to write, and I relied on family, friends, colleagues, acquaintances, and experts to candidly share their experiences and knowledge with me. First, I'd like to thank the wonderful folks at CPA Canada who entrusted me with a second book for the organization.

A special thank you to:

- Doretta Thompson, CPA Canada's Financial Literacy Leader, for all of your support, enthusiasm, and for always being a cheerleader;
- Li Zhang, Principal at CPA Canada, for that initial coffee where we envisioned *Uncoupling* and for giving me another shot at book writing; and
- Michael Massoud, CPA, CA, Principal at CPA Canada, for your constant support, trust in and patience with me.

I'd also like to thank the very talented professionals who took the time to chat and lent their expertise:

- Nora Spinks, chief executive officer and team lead, the Vanier Institute (Ottawa, ON);

- Rachel Margolis, demographer, sociologist, and associate professor in the department of sociology at Western University (London, ON);
- Sheri Spunt, attorney, Sheri M. Spunt, Avocats Inc. (Westmount, QC);
- Rosanne Walters, CPA, CA, CFE, CBV, Walters Financial Forensics (Delta, BC);
- Tanya Sterling, CPA, CA, CPCA, CFDS, CPC, Sterling Financial (Victoria, BC);
- Russell Alexander, attorney, founder, and senior partner, Russell Alexander Collaborative Family Lawyers (Lindsay, ON);
- Jessica Chapman, attorney, owner, Chapman Family Law (Dartmouth, NS);
- Renée le Nobel, CPA, CA, CFDS (Vancouver, BC);
- Kelly LaVallie, CPA, CA, CDFA, LaVallie & Associates Advisory Services Ltd. (Vancouver, BC);
- Lesley Kendall, lawyer, Law Society of Ontario Certified Specialist (Family Law), Cunningham, Swan, Carty, Little & Bonham LLP (Kingston, ON);
- Robynne Kazina, attorney, partner, Taylor McCaffrey LLP (Winnipeg, MB);
- Michael Deepwell, TEP, CPA, CA, CFP, CLU, Lamp Financial Inc.;
- Stefanie Ricchio-Forlingieri CPA, CGA, The Modern Accountant;
- Ted Wheatley, CPA, CGA, CFP;
- Sarah Mulhall, CPA, CA, Chartered Professional Accountants of Canada; and
- Rayna Shienfield, JD, Chartered Professional Accountants of Canada.

And a very heartfelt thank you to my friends and family for listening to me go on about divorce research and processes, and for all of your encouragement: many of my separated and divorced friends and colleagues, who were so candid and shared their stories without hesitation; my parents, Debbie and Alan Goldman, for showing Peter and I what a long-lasting marriage looks like; my husband, Peter, for supporting me as I wrote; and our kids, Addyson and Peyton, for (usually) letting me write in peace.

— *Lisa van de Geyn*

Special Acknowledgement

A special acknowledgment to Valarie Matthews, our technical reviewer. Valarie Matthews is a lawyer at McCarthy Hansen & Company LLP where she represents and advises clients on all issues related to the breakdown of relationships including parenting, spousal and child support, division of property, and separation agreements. She also advises and represents clients seeking marriage contracts or other domestic contracts. She is a graduate of Harvard Law School and holds a Bachelor of Business Administration degree with High Honors from the University of Georgia.

Valarie is an active member of the legal community as a mentor for Black Future Lawyers and the NCA Network, which is an organization for law students and lawyers in Canada who have degrees from international universities. Valarie also sits on the board of The June Callwood Centre for Young Women (Jessie's Centre) which provides educational and social supports for young people who are pregnant and parenting. She lives in Toronto with her husband, three children, and a dog named Moose.

About the Author

Lisa van de Geyn is an experienced, multi-award-winning journalist, magazine writer and editor. She's also the writer of the award-winning book *Babies: How to Afford Your Bundle of Joy*. She spends most of her time writing about women's issues, design, health and money for some of Canada's biggest magazines.

She graduated with a Bachelor of Journalism from Ryerson University (now Toronto Metropolitan University) in Toronto and has held positions at some of Canada's most celebrated publications, including *Chatelaine* and *Today's Parent*. She's also served as a writer and/or contributing editor at several magazines, including *Canadian Living*, *House & Home*, *Best Health*, *Living Luxe* and others.

Lisa is the mother of two teen and tween daughters, Addyson and Peyton. She lives just outside of Toronto and enjoys reading, listening to podcasts and her Netflix subscription.

We acknowledge the sacred land on which Cormorant Books operates. It has been a site of human activity for 15,000 years. This land is the territory of the Huron-Wendat and Petun First Nations, the Seneca, and most recently, the Mississaugas of the Credit River. The territory was the subject of the Dish With One Spoon Wampum Belt Covenant, an agreement between the Iroquois Confederacy and Confederacy of the Anishinaabe and allied nations to peaceably share and steward the resources around the Great Lakes. Today, the meeting place of Toronto is still home to many Indigenous people from across Turtle Island. We are grateful to have the opportunity to work in the community, on this territory.

We are also mindful of broken covenants and the need to strive to make right with all our relations.